Donna,
Thank you for improving my writing.
I enjoyed your class.

Leo Jacques

AFRICAN
Pearls AND
Poisons

AFRICAN
Pearls AND
Poisons

Idi Amin's Uganda; Kenya; Zaire's Pygmies

LEO LOUIS JACQUES

authorHOUSE®

AuthorHouse™
1663 Liberty Drive
Bloomington, IN 47403
www.authorhouse.com
Phone: 1-800-839-8640

Published by AuthorHouse   04/12/2013

ISBN: 978-1-4817-3272-7 (sc)
ISBN: 978-1-4817-3273-4 (e)

Library of Congress Control Number: 2013905535

DEDICATION

I dedicate this memoir to my love and wife of 55 years, Sue (Nee: Morton) for all her love, inspiration, research and reflections via diary keeping, in addition to her editing, photography and computer skills.

Sue's spunk and sureness, during difficult days, have been a super source of strength, to me. Sue's character makes her even more beautiful.

We, as a family of four, together, completed many long journeys (safaris). I believe our East and Central African Safaris are our most memorable, adventurous and veritable experiences we can share with you.

To our daughter, Laura Sue and her two children, Nicholas Scott and Charlotte Katherine, as well as, to our son, Kurtis Charles and his two sons, Ben Mathew and Carson Leo, we offer a small contribution to their family history, via this memoir, in words and photographs, with the prayer that they will follow our footsteps in appreciating World Humankind with love and sensitivity. We hope they will conserve all animals.

Our safaris (journeys) in Central and East Africa gained us some understanding and respect for the way Indigenous people live and survive through tumultuous times.

Adversity introduces a man to himself, and, as Disraeli pointed out, "There is no education like adversity." One surely has to be hard and hustle, in troublesome times.

I think we all learned something from our experiences in East and Central Africa.

We learned to respect the Indigenous Africans love for their land and their connection between mind, spirit and body. We learned that humankind deeply matters.

We hope our safaris display good feelings for humankind through our relationships with different cultures. We went to help those less fortunate than ourselves and learned a lot about living from those we became friends and co-partners with.

I understand we live our lives positively forward, yet read it positively and negatively backwards, thus experiencing pearls (goods) and poisons (evils).

Therefore, one cannot judge the completion of my objective only by its success or failure, but by the effort put forth to build a framework for others to follow and complete, in a relatively more rational time.

The Indigenous African speaks Swahili, saying, "Usikunbake uovu ukasahau fadhila," which, in English, means, "Make judgment, based on both:—pearl and poisons, in everything."

ACKNOWLEDGEMENTS

My wife, Sue (PHT.) provided all the pictures for this book by taking some great images of Uganda, Kenya and Zaire. I am GRATEFUL for all the priceless help that you, Sue have provided to me in making this book possible and plausible.

A SPECIAL THANKS goes to Darcy Nybo (Madam C.O.W.) for her steady and continual encouragement of me to write on the Jacques family's East African Safari experiences, as well as adding her insightful critiques, at the Central Okanagan Writing Society (C.O.W.S.), at the Dragon's Lair, in West Kelowna. I would also like to RECOGNIZE the other scribes of C.O.W.S. for their critical comments, as well as their warm friendships.

I am also DEEPLY INDEBTED to the Senior's Learning in Retirement (S.L.R.) "Let's Write" Leader and Wordsmith, Susanna Svendsen, as well as S.L.R's "Let's Write" Co-Leaders, Leah Todd and Jean Christenson. For five years, these authors led groups, of amicable and dedicated writers, in critiquing my book, chapter-by-chapter, paragraph-by-paragraph, and line-by-line. They helped me find my voice. Please accept my INDEBTEDNESS.

I am APPRECIATIVE to anyone, who has read my work: for his or her critiques, analysis and friendship. You know who you are, and my TRIBUTES emit too you.

THANK YOU each and every one of you.

You helpers are VALUED in making my memoir safaris joyously possible for you, the reader.

OTHER BOOKS WRITTEN BY THIS AUTHOR

Leo Louis wrote two acclaimed Thoroughbred horseracing books:

Call to the Post:—Johnny Longden's Glories and Goofs (AuthorHouse)

And

JOEY:—Calgary's Horse and Racing's Hall of Famers (Puckshot Press).

Leo Louis Jacques has also written:

Non-Fiction books:

The Self-Employed Business,

Oil In Central Alberta,

Sports Writing and Creative Non-Fiction,

"Youbetcha"—The Thoroughbred Will Win.

Children books:

Toytown Express (Non-Fiction)

Young Writer's Various Ways of Training a Horse (Non-Fiction)

Poetry Books:

Freestyling with Eyes Wide Shut

Happy/Sad Poems with Heart

Love of Hockey & Horse Poetry

Haiku for Hockey, Horses and Hounds

Mybestoyou

TABLE OF CONTENTS

FOREWORD...xix

PREFACE..xxi

CHAPTER ONE

READYING FOR PEARL OF AFRICA 1

    SAFARI 1...1

    SAFARI 2...9

    SAFARI 3...14

CHAPTER TWO

UGANDA IS AN AFRICAN PEARL......................................16

    SAFARI 4...16

    SAFARI 5...27

    SAFARI 6...39

    SAFARI 7...53

    SAFARI 8...66

    SAFARI 9...77

    SAFARI 10...81

CHAPTER THREE

COMINGS AND GOINGS-ON...92

    SAFARI 11...92

    SAFARI 12...97

    SAFARI 14...105

    SAFARI 15...112

CHAPTER FOUR

KENYA IS WORLD'S SAFARI CAPITAL..............................118

    SAFARI 16...118

SAFARI 17..129

SAFARI 18..135

SAFARI 19..145

SAFARI 20..154

SAFARI 21..165

SAFARI 22..171

SAFARI 23..179

SAFARI 24..189

SAFARI 25..195

CHAPTER FIVE

COOL MOUNTAINS OF THE MOON 202

SAFARI 26..202

SAFARI 27..208

SAFARI 28..222

SAFARI 29..228

SAFARI 30..240

CHAPTER SIX

ZAIRE HAD PYGMY PEARLS 249

SAFARI 31..249

CHAPTER SEVEN

GAME PARK PEARLS AD POISONS 259

SAFARI 32..259

SAFARI 33..267

SAFARI 34..279

SAFARI 35..291

CHAPTER EIGHT

MEDICAL PEARLS AND POISONS 303

    SAFARI 36..303

CHAPTER NINE

CLOSE-CALL POISONS 310

    SAFARI 37..310

CHAPTER TEN

POISONS PILE-UP, TO PARTING 319

    SAFARI 38..319

    SAFARI 39..336

    SAFARI 40..355

CHAPTER ELEVEN

CUT-ADRIFT BY CLOAK-AND-DAGGER 371

    SAFARI 41..371

    SAFARI 42..382

EPILOGUE 393

OUR FAVORITE DISHES 403

SWAHILI RIDDLES..409

LIST OF PICTURES

01. "AFFAIR OF THE HAIR:"—SUE AND LAURA, IN THEIR HOME-MADE KITENGE DRESSES, IN SAMS' BACKYARD....................8

02. "FRIENDS HOLDING HANDS"—K.C. AND DERRICK, IN BACKYARD OF OUR PROPERTY, AT COLLEGE. 38

03. "'RED CARPET GUESTS:"—IDI AND KAY AMIN, WELCOMED AT COLLEGE.'"....................65

04. "AN UNCROWDED BEACH:"—LAURA AND K.C., IN WHITE SAND, ON MOMBASSA BEACH..................177

05. "INDIAN OCEAN BREEZES:"—LEO AND K.C., IN KITENGE SHIRTS, BEHIND GERMAN HOTEL, IN MALINDI. 178

06. "SUE AND GROUP OF ZAIRE'S TWA PYGMIES, OF THE ITURI RAINFOREST."....................257

07. "A HAPPY GANG OF ZAIRE'S TWA PYGMIES, OF THE ITURI RAINFOREST."....................258

08. "LOOKING FOR TROUBLE:"—CAPE BUFFALO, THAT SURROUNDED OUR CAR, SCOUTING TO STAMPEDE. 277

09. "BIG FELLAS"—HIPPO AND CROC,
IN VICTORIA NILE RIVER...278

10. "SEE YA:"—A FAMILY OF FOUR ELEPHANTS,
LEAVE IN A HURRY," 391

FOREWORD

I feel privileged to write the foreword to this fine East and Central African expeditionary memoir by fellow and award winning author, Leo Louis Jacques.

The Jacques family's safaris passed through some of the most breathtaking—often life threatening—landscapes and situations, on earth. Leo's eyes light up, shoulders straighten and voice rises when he talks and writes about these safaris.

He writes well about these places, where his family of four went to serve:—by way of being temporarily transferred from Calgary, Canada to another country on another continent. Having arrived there, they extensively journeyed within the East African countries of Uganda and Kenya as well as visiting the Twa Pygmies in Zaire.

Leo's compelling comments and content on 1970's Uganda, Kenya and Zaire are like sweeping your arm across an atlas to clear your fertile mind and elicit images, feelings and understandings. I drank the wild African air with the Jacques family, as they looked a tragicomic Despot's danger in the eye and persevered, in a valiant attempt, to fulfill their commitment.

I devoured Leo's book in two sittings and was greatly saddened when it came to an end. His vivid descriptions and narrative arc kept me on the edge of my seat and widened my horizons. Leo's African experiences and resulting memoir are more interesting than anything I've ever witnessed or written.

If you desire an interesting and exhilarating account of Uganda, Kenya and the nomadic pygmies of Zaire, then this book's for you. Enjoy!

Yours truly,

MacDonald Coleman, Author

PREFACE

Welcome to my happy/sad adventurous memoir of "our <u>safaris</u>" to a string of African nations that persisted in pitching pearls and poisons.

Our family of four was housed in a compound, with askaris (guards), at the Uganda College of Commerce in the Nakawa District of Kampala, Uganda, East Africa, under the rule of President Idi Amin:—from August 15, 1971 to November 30, 1972.

My serving at the Uganda College of Commerce as the Head of the Departments:—Business and Distributive (Sales & Marketing) Education, Tourism and Household Economics & Catering, caused me to become unemployed.

The contract didn't last the full two years and here's the story why.

I will try to shed some light on how Canada prepared us; good and bad things that happened to us; and why our government had us hurriedly exiting Uganda, after British Intelligence Officers had rescued me from killers: and had me signing a contract not to write a book about Uganda for 40 years, as well as never to return to this pearl of Africa.

After many years of mulling things over in my mind, and also some dreams and nightmares, I wrote this memoir. It took a long time for me to get this story out to you.

PLEASE NOTE:—I HAVE CHANGED THE SURNAMES OF ALL NON-FAMILY PEOPLE INVOLVED IN THIS MEMOIR SO AS TO NOT INFRINGE ON THEIR PRIVACY AND/OR HURT ANYONE'S FEELINGS.

While centered in Kampala's Nakawa District, we traveled extensively in Kampala and throughout Uganda, Kenya, as well as into the Ituri Rainforest of Zaire.

As an educator, journalist, artist and author, I kept lessons, notes, paintings and pictures of our experiences during these years, as well as correspondence from the human beings who remained in war torn Uganda. I hope my memoir can enlighten you as to what we saw and how we felt during this time period.

My wife of thirteen years, Sue (Nee: Morton)—33 years old, and I—35, with our daughter, Laura—12, and son, K.C.—3, found Uganda, Kenya and Zaire, to be pearls mixed with a growing poisonous build up during our years in these countries' boundaries.

During our time in Uganda, each member of our family would gain an extensive outlook on the world and would suffer a serious ailment. As a family of four, we nearly "bought the farm (died)" once. Some friends and acquaintances:—not so lucky.

Death, injuries and emotional scars were not from those who were bitten dead by some of the most poisonous snakes and/or spiders in the world or killed, or maimed by African wildlife, including the 'Big Five.'

Why did some of Uganda's, Kenya's and Zaire's pearls turn to poison for their Indigenous, us expatriates and some tourists, during these years? Why did so many martyrs die heroes? How did East African Socialism affect our Safaris?

The word, "Safari," in Swahili, is more than goggling at Africa's many wild animals. In Swahili, "Safari" simply means "Journey:"—a word used to say we are traveling far away.

I wrote my memoir, in the Swahili's "Safari" divisions, under the "Chapter" groupings, because my memoir was made up of many "Journeys" our family experienced in East and Central Africa. The "Safaris," composing "Pearls/Poisons" pitched in Uganda, Kenya and Zaire, are not all in chronological order. Some of the Chapters are in "a related Safari" sequence, so as to cover the commonality of these Safaris (voyages). One and one, doesn't always equal two. My memoir is what it is!

CHAPTER ONE
READYING FOR PEARL OF AFRICA

<u>SAFARI 1</u>

My memoir is mainly about my account of our family's feelings and encounters, while dwelling in Uganda, Kenya and Zaire in 1971 and 1972, and the consequences of serving in a country, governed by a tyrant and correspondence from those who stayed. These reminiscences include many kinds and sizes of human beings, wild beasts, as well as supernatural scenery, while we were on many safaris within Equatorial East and Central Africa.

This is true tale of a tropical pearl of a paradise that was poisoned by a diabolical lunatic and his followers, while I, Leo, with my photographer wife, Sue, as well as daughter, Laura and son, K.C., resided there and some of the telling effects these supernatural places had on us and others.

Here's my opening verse that a bard could possibly spin into a poignant poem:

SO LONG, CALGARY,

CITY REARED IN.

SO LONG, EDMONTON,

POST-SECONDARY ED.

SO LONG WINNIPEG,

ACCOUNT, AUDIT TRAINING.

SUPPORTIVE WIFE BACKS

INTERNATIONAL DREAM.

OH, THE TELEPHONE RANG,

RANG OFF THE WALL,

WAS OTTAWA MAKING A CALL?

THEIR TIME EIGHT,

OURS FIVE.

MY EYES SLITS,

BUT I STILL HAD JIVE.

TWAS A LADY NAMED PORTER,

ASKING ME TO SERVE

IN UGANDA, EAST AFRICA:

"IF I HAD THE NERVE."

I COVERED THE PHONE

ASKED WIFE:—"WHERE?"

"JUST SAY YES, IT'S NO HALLOWEEN DARE."

PORTER, "NEXT WEEK, TO EDMONTON GO:

SIGN UP, ORIENTATE AND STOW

THINGS IN COMPOUND NEAR

'CAUSE YOU'RE IN AFRICA FALL, THIS YEAR."

SO LONG, CALGARY,

GOOD EARNING AND LIVING.

SO LONG, EDMONTON,

TOP VARSITY PROFS.

SO LONG, WINNIEPOOPEG,

BIZ LINGO LEARNED.

AU REVOIR, OTTAWA,

BILINGUAL CAPITAL.

AFT THIRD WORLD INDOC,

  BROWSING LONDON, TRIPOLI'S SHORES,

  ALIT ENTEBBE TO KAMPALA, UGANDA

  HUMANKIND CRADLE,

  TO JOURNEY NEXT DUO YEARS.

  UGANDA NEEDS US TO SERVE THEM.

  NOW SCRIBING SAFARI EXPERIENCES.

It was May 25, 1971, the morning after my wife, Sue's 33rd birthday. The next week, we arranged for a nanny to baby-sit our two children, Laura and K.C., as went to Edmonton to sign a two year contract that seconded (aid for another place) me from the Provincial

Government of Alberta to the Federal Government of Canada (C.I.D.A.) to the 2nd Republic of Uganda, to be stationed at the Uganda College of Commerce for two years from August 31, 1971 until August 31, 1973, with a five years renewal option.

The Canadian International Development Agency (C.I.D.A.) had been formed in 1968 to offer Canada's Official Development Assistance (O.D.A.) to reduce poverty, promote human rights and support sustainable development.

The Canadian International Development Agency (C.I.D.A.) would be my paying employer and the Ugandan government would be my boss.

C.I.D.A. deemed my experiences, with Canadian Indians (First Nations) at the Alberta Morley Reserve and the Eskimos (Inuits) in Norman Wells, N.W.T. and Uranium City, Saskatchewan, as well as our family's extensive camping experiences in the Pacific Northwest, useful to living and supporting sustainable development in a Third World Nation like Uganda.

C.I.D.A.'s Catrina Porter said, "Your work with Reserve Indians and the Northern Eskimos and your family's spirit and co-operation are necessary incidences to live in unfamiliar settings and getting along with peoples from these other developing places."

She added, "I'm impressed with your willingness, as a family, to travel to a Third World country to help those less fortunate than yourselves. I think you are made of the pioneering spirit that will make us all proud to be Canadians."

My cheques were deposited in our Canadian bank account, with drawing privileges that had to be set up at Barclay of London's, Kampala, Uganda branch, once we got to the capital of this East African Country.

This contract entailed moving our family of four from Calgary to Kampala. Our family longhaired dachshund dog, Janie was given to Sue's girlfriend, Jezebel. Shortly after we left Canada, Janie passed on. The family cars and holiday trailer were sold. Our home was rented out and its contents stored with a security firm. We bought a washer and stove, with the proper wiring, and had them included in our sea shipment.

Porter said, "To ensure that you are not having any additions to your family while in Africa, one of you has to be sterilized.

Your doctor has to provide to us a document with proof that the sterilization operation has taken place."

CIDA's Catrina Porter and Ronald Wood would act, as our Canadian liaison officers and both, or one of the two, were said to be in Uganda to welcome us.

In Ottawa, I had asked Ms. Porter, "There was a change in the government of Uganda in January of this year was there not? How will it affect us?"

Porter answered, "Yes, there was a coup on January 25th, 1971 and it was a move that promises to be an improvement. The new administration favors Democracy and Western Civilization's Democracy, while the former one favored the Communists."

I said, "I understand the present government being run by the Ugandan army under the control of a General named Idi Amin Dada. What is he like?"

Porter said, "General Amin's gone on record as saying:—he loves Canada and the Commonwealth. He also vowed that his country of Uganda would have democratic elections soon. The British and

Americans have recognized him as the Ugandan government and so do we."

A house was to be provided for us at the Uganda College of Commerce compound, where I believed, I was to serve as a Business Administration Instructor.

Since the cost of this rental house would be minimal, we were expected to clean it all up after the Indigenous African family, that was presently living in it, moved to a newer and cleaner house.

This was a common way of refurbishing houses in Kampala:—having an African family, then a European (White) family living in a house, in that order.

We were expected to hire Indigenous African servants so that our money would be spread around in the community in which we were living.

Based on my personal creed:—"We pass this way but once," I wanted to make a positive difference to the people of Uganda and display how hard a Canadian can work for their betterment and fulfill C.I.D.A.'s manifesto.

"AFFAIR OF THE HAIR:"—SUE AND LAURA, IN THEIR
HOME-MADE KITENGE DRESSES, IN SAMS' BACKYARD.

SAFARI 2

On August 1, 1971, Sue and I went to Ottawa, to be involved in an intensive Third World Brainwashing and Indoctrination Training Session at Carlton University. Catrina Porter acted as our Liaison Officer.

The sessions at Carlton were intended to be our preparation for living in an African Culture and help us survive in a Third World Nation.

Sue was sent to one Life-Simulated Survival Group and I was sent to a different one. Neither of us knew what to expect, although I had experienced indoctrination training in the "Dog-Eat-Dog" Intentional Brainwashing Techniques the Chinese Government had used on American Prisoners of War (P.O.W.'s) during the Korean War.

The Communists had used sociological and psychological methods, in an attempt to get American P.O.W.'s to turn on each other and take away everything from their weakest link:—"because they weren't going to need anything much longer." Big Brother watched and bit-by-bit tried to change the mores of the young Americans.

Our C.I.D.A. Survival Groups would be simulatively marooned on an island out in the ocean, or a desolate mountain, with no provisions. Each group had to find ways to survive, much like some of the T.V. reality shows of today's year.

Each Survival Group consisted of eight people:—four men and four women. Each Group, had to have:—one Philosopher King or Queen, one Warrior and six Service Persons:—a Homemaker, a Child Bearer, a Cook, a Hunter/Food Gatherer, a Fish Provider and a General Laborer.

The Philosopher King/Queen would plan what had to be done; the Warrior would be the defenders of the group; and the Service People would do what was assigned to them by the Philosopher King/Queen, such as help fight and defend, generate kids, etc.:—"For the good of the group, so help you God."

Everyone ate sparingly, with his or her group and after a long, long day, we fell exhausted into their dormitory beds at Carlton University.

It was a test of everyone's survival skills, as none of us group members knew each other before the Life-Simulation Exercises that went on for 12 hours a day for 12 continuous days. It got to the point where many of the participants started to live the assignment and there were three participants who quit the exercise and their posting.

I recall, as a Warrior, being commanded by my Philosopher King to repel the other group's attacks on our Hunter/Food Gatherer, Fish Provider and Child Bearer.

It was a mentally, emotionally, as well as physically, challenging and draining experience. There were a total of ten attacks on our Group by two other competing groups. All sides shed lots of blood. I had two badly skinned knees and elbows from being forcefully thrown down a stairwell by Group "B." Outside of my own Group, one didn't know whom one could really trust.

On being re-united with Philosopher Queen, Sue on day 13, we were introduced to the Swahili language. We also sampled the East African cuisine provided by C.I.D.A. as well as meeting with other couples who had already served abroad. We didn't meet anyone who had served in Africa. Most of the alumni there had served in the Caribbean.

Before our time in Ottawa ended, we met, under unusual circumstances, our next room neighbors, Wally and Nona Sams of Edmonton.

I was shaving at the bathroom mirror when it swung open and Wally's face appeared before me as he yelled, "Mona! Help me Mona!" just like the Gillette blade commercial currently running on T.V.

We all laughed, while introducing ourselves. The Sams were to serve in Masindi, Uganda. Wally was a High School Science Department Head and Science Teacher at Ross Shepard High School in Edmonton. We had met when we were both students on the campus of the University of Alberta in the 1964/65 years.

On our last day at Carlton, Sue and I walked ten blocks to Lansdowne Park to watch a Canadian Football League game between the two Rough Rider—Roughrider teams, Ottawa and Saskatchewan, respectively. We were fortunate to have kindly strangers pick us up just outside the stadium gates and drive us back to Carlton.

At length, we discussed our impressions of the brainwashing sessions and felt that it had helped us to understand some of the language, customs and conditions under which we were to serve, as well as our place in the broader scheme of things.

We returned to Calgary in high spirits. I recall saying to our two children, "Ottawa is one great city. It has so much Canadian history." Sue added, "Yes, and they have real nice people and a good football club."

It was now time to attend to the last minute details. Sue closed our plastic accounts. Both of us were parentless—mine having passed on in the 1950's and Sue's in the 1960's. She has a younger brother, Phil. I, have a younger brother, Joe and an elder sister, Suzanne (Sue).

Only one person said he was against our going to Uganda, East Africa

SAFARI 3

We were getting ready to taxi off to the airport, to fly to London, on our way to Africa when the telephone rang, rang and rang till it nearly shook itself off the hook.

I said, "Hello. Yes Sir.

Sue, it's Uncle Graham. Yes, we're going . . . Okay, I'll get her."

I covered the phone with my hand and said, "Don't be long. We're running a little late."

"Hi, Uncle Graham," said Sue. "What can I do for you?"

"Sue, don't go! Don't go to Africa," said Graham Morton, a 60 year-old, who was head of Calgary's most successful Chartered Accounting (C.P.A.) firm.

"Why, Uncle Graham? What are your concerns?"

"Africa is a long ways away and Uganda is an unstable country."

"But, we've been assured by Ottawa that it's much safer now under its new regime," said Sue.

"Sue—your folks would roll over in their graves if they knew what you were doing," said Graham. "Has your daring, young husband signed a contract?"

"Yes, we're signed on for two years. I do wish you'd have phoned sooner. Right now, we're on our way to the airport to Winnipeg, then to go over the pole to London."

"Just remember, you get yourself and your two children out of that country if you see any signs of war or killings, Sue. Do you understand?"

"Yes, Uncle Graham. Thank you. Thank you for . . ."

"Click."

Sue said, "'Bye, Uncle Graham."

It would be the last time she would hear his deep, firm voice.

CHAPTER TWO
UGANDA IS AN AFRICAN PEARL

SAFARI 4

On August 23, 1971, we flew via Canadian Pacific Air (nicknamed 'See Pierre,' after our then Prime Minister, Pierre Trudeau) from Calgary to Edmonton to Winnipeg and over the North Pole to London, England.

In order to break up the long air trip to Uganda, we spent one week at London's Crystal Palace Hotel, across from the Piccadilly Circus traffic circle.

It was risking one's life not to heed London's hectic traffic, but we survived and visited highlights of the birth city of my now deceased dad, Charles Louis Jacques. I nodded off on some of our educational sightseeing tours.

Sue took charge of Laura and K.C., and said, "Leo, you wear yourself out."

I thought: I'm still playing C.I.D.A.'s 'Warrior role.'

Africa was next. We saw the tip of it from our British United Airways jet as it touched down for refueling in Tripoli, Libya, where it was 105 degrees Fahrenheit.

Five, armed Libyan soldiers boarded the plane searching for arms and munitions in the aisles and under our seats. Their leader, with a loud grunt, brushed his gun under my legs and abruptly lifted it upwards causing me to grunt, too. There was no love in the eyes of that soldier. All five of them had their guns drawn and ready to fire.

Our silver British airliner circled above the shore of Lake Victoria, banked, turned and glided down on invisible runway tarmac, surrounded by water, to thump on the tufty grass of the Entebbe, Uganda Airport.

We jarringly taxied on jagged pieces of concrete to the terminal building. We gawked out the small windows at what was to be our new residence.

From the air, we'd seen: lots of greenery, red earth and buildings with thatched roofs. Masses of people were moving around on wonky bicycles, overloaded buses, and battered lorries (trucks). There were also safari vans, yet the majority of the people were on foot. Market places seem to be at every corner lot.

Now, we were going to experience our new abode closer up. The doors of our 'big bird' flew open like a robin's nib.

As we were trying to exit through those doors, there was a commotion at the front of the plane's exiting line.

From what I could make out:—a young, British man in his twenties was yelling, "We will not get off this plane. I demand we be returned to London right away."

The friendly, young, blond steward was trying his best to appease the man and his equally young female companion. The steward kept saying, "Please stand aside so as to let the rest of the passengers disembark."

The young Brit tartly said to me, "There are too many blacks here for our liking. We insist on being returned to London, right away."

After a seemingly very long queue time, we emerged from the plane to see what had disturbed this couple so much.

We saw black people moving against the backdrop of palm trees. We smelled the musty wildness in the air that we had never experienced before. We heard loud noises from these indigenous:—yelling, toiling and ever smiling while working with massive machinery, near the backdrop of the encompassing rainforest growth.

I thought:—What's wrong with that couple demanding to return to London? There was a variety of indigenous skin shades:—from copper to chocolate, from ochre to brown then to the deepest ebony:—that makes nonsense to the single word "black" to describe their color. The beautiful people of Uganda are black, but not too black. They are brown, but not too brown. They surely love to attire in bright red and gold colors.

Entebbe lies curled round the lakeshore in a green amphitheater, shaded with huge old trees, domed mango trees, flame-flowered tulip trees, scarlet and flamboyant jacaranda trees, incense and fig trees, and the tall muvuli, known as the African teak tree.

I smelled a rank wildness in the air. It was like the odor of a closed cattle barn. My breathing became shallow and I would eventually lost inches from around my chest.

Entebbe is lush with tree growth and has a smell of its own:—wild, challenging and inviting. It was like the equatorial jungle the Tarzan movies were produced in.

The intoxicating beauty of Entebbe's massive, outside rooted trees affected us so, that we asked our friend Nona Sam to grab onto one of the giant vines, that hung down, and act like Tarzan's Jane: climb and swing on it.

Nona weighed about as much as a steeplechase jockey.

We all chanted, "The vine, Jane, the vine!"

Being a good sport, Nona ran her fingers over the vine and started her upward climb. When she was three or four feet up, she made a giant swing. A loud snap shattered the silence and down she came to the turf with a thump.

Tears came to her eyes and empathy emerged. Not one picture was taken of the incident. We all expressed our deep sorrow for brave Nona.

We later learned that the terrified couple had remained on the plane had been put on the next plane bound for Europe:—most likely London.

There are fruits everywhere. The small bananas are a staple called mutoke that taste and are prepared like a potato by the indigenous cooks.

We also learned that Ugandans are sensitive to their different shades of skin color, which may denote tribal origins.

Tribalism is based on "territorial imperative" and power. It is not savage or primitive. A tribe is an ethnically homogeneous group possessing a 'first' language (e.g. Swahili, Luganda), thus unique to them. It also shows the site of their ancestral origin.

Within the tribe is a guttural, shorthand speech—a restricted code form of communication—of that tribe. The unique customs and history of the tribe allow members to have a conversation:—consisting mostly of little sayings:—no more than proverbs and riddles.

Examples are: "It's a beautiful day, but the river is red with blood." Or, "The bull elephant always has the right of way." Or, "Don't wade in a hungry croc's river."

Any tribal member, who wishes to avoid penetration by other collective groups, such as us, will fall back on this restricted language code.

Against a backdrop of swaying palm trees, I heard loud conversations in Swahili from the African Indigenous people.

At times, we felt fenced out of the 'information loop' the Ugandans were in. After all, we weren't Indigenous to the area and were considered Expatriates not Tourists.

When we lived in Uganda, the population was ten million—mostly rural folk. Kampala (330,000) was the only city, although Jinja town had 60,000 people.

For every 10,000 African Black Indigenous Persons there were 100 East African Indians and one White. Uganda's Black majority is called the African Indigenous people. In 1971, East African Indians were 99 per cent of Uganda's business faction.

Hence, 99 per cent of the remaining one per cent was made up of Musongu (White):—are all grouped together, in the classification—European. Musongu is the Swahili word for a headless chicken that runs around haphazardly in circles.

This Musongu word for a White might have come from the Indigenous who witnessed the British men in emergency experiences. The British men who would roll up their sleeves and scurry around giving orders to everyone within "earshot." The Brits called It:—"Getting the essential things done in the quickest, correct way and manner."

Being in the microscopic minority was a new, unique experience for us, as a North American family, and at a big challenge for each of us.

Each member tried very hard to fit in and remain upbeat about serving in Uganda.

Within a few weeks, we felt more comfortable with our living situation:—Where we were? What we were doing? What we felt we could offer? How we fit in? How can we survive and contribute more?

I was proud of our family's positive attitude to Africa, a region of the world that is sometimes called, 'the Lost Continent,' even though it's the World's second largest continent and second most populated place and has the longest history of human activity.

Historians point out: "With its present population growth of seven children per family, Uganda will be the 15th most populated country in the world, by the year, 2050."

Uganda's largest tribe was the Bugandans. The Bugandans spoke Lugandan, English and Swahili. The Bugandans had called the country Uganda—Swahili for 'Land of the Ganda.' The name in Lugandan for their king was the Kabaka.

In 1966, Uganda's first President, Sir Edward (Kabaka King Freddie) Mutesa II had been routed out by the then Army Commander, Idi Amin Dada on the orders of the then Prime Minister, Milton Apollo Obote. Then, Obote named himself President.

King Freddie escaped through Burundi to exile in London, where he had remained until his suspicious, liquor related death in 1969. It was suspected that he was poisoned. Before his death in London, King Freddie had vowed, "I shall return to the land of my father and my people."

The Bugandan tribe wanted to bury "their King" at the Kabaka Tombs, near his thatched-roofed palatial residence where his seven wives and his extended family lived.

I recalled, back in Ottawa, Catrina Porter saying, "I believe the matter of burying King Freddie's body at the Kabaka Tombs in Kampala is presently being considered by the Ugandan government."

On April 12, 1971, with President Amin's approval (after he had dissolved parliament with no future elections), King Freddie had been buried, with full honors, at the Kabaka Tombs.

On September 2, 1971, on a special invite, our family visited the tombs. Sue took some pictures and bought colorful baskets from King Freddie's many wives and extended family.

When we visited the Kabaka Tombs, King Freddie's wives and their brood continued to live at the Tombs, while being fed by the Bugandan tribe of Uganda.

The Bugandan men liked their women plump. They believed it to be a show of their (the man's) prosperity. One Bugandan man said to me, "It also makes for a 'lotta' woman to grab hold of."

SAFARI 5

Uganda is 236,040 square kilometers, in size. British Columbia is 994,186 square kilometers, in dimensions. Minnesota is 221,181 square kilometers, large.

Why would a Country (Uganda), not as large as one-quarter of the Province of B.C., but a bit bigger than the State of Minnesota, become known as "a pearl"?

Uganda lies in the middle of Africa with the equator cutting it into two equal parts—a wilder, northerly part and a more densely populated, tamer southerly part.

This mainly rurally populated country had fields after fields (savannas) of lush green Nile grass.

An old muzee (revered) Ugandan said, "Dig a small hole with a table fork, plant a seed of anything and it will grow abundantly overnight. Any kind of plant, shrub or crop can be grown here. That is why we can live in huts, even on a mountain side."

I overheard an American traveler say, "Entebbe is like the Garden of Eden. During October, the season of the short rains, it's a lush green as if drenched in crème de menthe."

The peninsula on which Entebbe stands is a favorite resting place for migrating birds. Probably no other spot in Uganda has such a vast show of birds swooping and fluttering from tree to tree: Yellow Weaver birds, Shrikes, Scarlet and Black Honeysuckers, Flashing Blue Kingfishers, Starlings, Jays, Swallows, Wagtails and Chats. It's a birdwatcher's paradise.

A full chorus of twittering song heralds the dawn here. The honking of the Republic's bird, the Golden-Crested Crane, as it flies to its nesting place in some tall muvuli tree, breaking the quiet of the evening. These Crested Cranes are thought to be, "the birds of heaven," because they fly so high and for that reason are included in Uganda's flag and on her currency.

Crows, in clerical black and white, squawk in the gardens. Grey Herons, White Egrets and Fish Eagles perch, brood and swoop on the lake's edge, while Hawks, Condors and Buzzards wheel and hover against the milky blue of the sky.

Visitors arrive and depart daily from Entebbe's airport. Arrivals then go every which way, stopping for unique souvenirs, taking photographs of the Black Indigenous African peoples, observing the wonderful wildlife and tropical richness, as well as noticing the marks civilization has made upon Uganda.

Humankind first emerged in East Africa, shown by the fossils found by the Leakey's and others as well as with evidence recently bolstered by DNA studies.

Religion holds a special spot in East and Central African culture. There are hundreds of African Indigenous religions with multiplicity of deities and spirits, yet there has been an impact of the two great World Religions:—Christianity and Islam.

The most profound connection between North America and East and Central Africa is, without a doubt, the forced migration of a large number of African slaves for permanent residence in the New World.

The Indian Ocean provided the means by which the entrapped East African slaves were first taken, via the Cape of Good Hope, to West Africa. Then, those that survived the safari were transported to the New World just three decades after Christopher Columbus founded North America.

The 1800's brought the abilities of the Atlantic slave traders and the onset of European colonization.

In 1884, representation of several Western civilization powers met in Berlin and discussed the ground rules in the "Scramble for Africa," and these European nations were highly motivated with the search for raw materials and new markets, the missionary impulse and pseudoscientific notions of racial superiority.

Uganda had made a late appearance on the map of Africa. This entire continent had been known as "Dark or Lost."

Indeed, authentic records of the history of Uganda began only when J.H. Speke, with his companion, J.H. Grant reached the court of Mutesa, the Kabaka (King) of Buganda, in 1862.

Later, in that same year, Speke discovered Ripon Falls, near Jinja town and mistakenly thought it to be the source of the Nile River.

In 1901, explorer, Richard Speke was the first white person to call Uganda, "the Pearl of Africa."

Previously, Arab traders and slavers from Kenya's white-sanded, Indian Ocean coastal ports of Mombassa, Masindi and Lamu had penetrated as far as Uganda in their raids (for ivory and slaves), according to the few records that existed at that time.

One can think back to when the first missionaries arrived, in response to Sir Henry M. Stanley's famous appeal in London's Daily Telegraph newspaper headline entitled, "See the Great African Lake."

The lake he was referring to was Lake Victoria, the World's second largest freshwater lake. Stanley copied Speke by also calling Uganda, "the Pearl of Africa." He was smitten with Uganda's beauty!

Over 100 years ago, missionary journeys to Uganda took six months to complete. They would walk up from the Indian Ocean's coast, with their food and belongings borne on the woolly heads of Swahili porters, while they themselves often rode on the backs of the pack donkeys.

In those days, the crossing of Lake Victoria was made in canoes of sewn planks, sketchily equipped with broad-bladed paddles, some gourds for baling and overtures to the gods in the form of a few fluttering rags or plantain leaves at the prow. The Arabs used small dhows to navigate, "the big lake."

Imagine what the early Uganda visitors faced:—hostile tribes, fevers, tropical diseases, torrential rains, violent lake storms, drought, and man-eating lions, that prowled by night round their camps.

Most of the European residents living in Uganda returned to their country of origin like home plants bedded out for a time in a tropical garden. They are expatriates and aliens in a foreign land. No amount of exposure to global worldliness will ever make Uganda a white man's country.

Historically, Uganda resembles a natural, black pearl. Its core has always been black and the pearl comes as a result of the struggle to stay that way. This African country was never colonized like Kenya and other African countries. The British held it as a protectorate.

The East African lion awoke. There was a rise in nationalism in the 20th Century came in two forms: Indigenous Africans protested to claim back their land in the form such as the 1950's Mau Mau rebellion in Kenya against colonial Great Britain in which the dubbed terrorists plundered and killed white European settlers during dark nights.

The other nationalistic viewpoint took the form of looking forward to a new East Africa, different from both the pre-colonial and colonial models.

The two models co-existed and overlapped in East African nations like Uganda and Kenya. The peaceful path to independence in Uganda took place in 1961, when the British protectorate became free. In Kenya, it wasn't until 1963 that the Kenya colony became an independent nation.

In Uganda, we will never forget:—Indigenous African people:—happy and seemingly well adjusted with an annual income of $162; slim, nearly seven foot tall tribesmen with profiles like Egyptian frescoes; pygmies, living like gypsies, in the primeval rainforest; jungle-story beasts:—apes, baboons, monkeys, giraffes, tree climbing lions, leopards, cheetahs, rhinos, hippos, elephants, cape buffaloes, crocodiles, snakes, spiders, lizards and all kinds of tropical birds.

There were backdrops:—silvery lakes and giant volcanoes, deep crater lakes, green and mysterious. The ancient Nile flowing placidly hurling itself over rugged, magnificent falls; seeing snow atop the Mountains of the Moon, at the Equator; grass that grew high above one's head; rustling bamboo forests; great plains with all sizes of shrubs and gigantic, ten-foot tall anthills.

If you were to visit for three weeks, Uganda could display, for you, most of its peoples, animals, landscapes and mirages. There are drivable roads all over the country, albeit mostly narrow, twisted and rutted, among the bamboo forests and volcanoes. You can also take a ride on "Lake Vic" or the Nile in a yacht or comfortable riverboat.

It's when you actually live in Uganda, as a resident or expatriate, and not as a tourist (short-term visitor), that you see something more intricate and revealing about the country. You see its heart and soul.

It is then; the "pearls" and the "poisons" seep out.

The people and animals that live in East and Central Africa are amazing.

When you queue up for anything, be it for banking or for a dreaded tetanus shot, three lines form: one for the tourists, one for the expatriates and one for the indigenous.

Guess which one of the three is treated best? Yes, the tourist line. It is the tourist that brings in the much-needed foreign currency to the country of Uganda.

The expatriates and indigenous get treated not as well, in fact, sometimes dreadfully.

We Canadians have a tendency to talk a lot about the weather.

Unlike Canada, Uganda's weather is predictable most of the time so you appear as being "odd" if you talk about it too much. We learned that in a hurry.

In the morning it's misty and wet; by mid-day it's hot; by 2 p.m. It's humid, by 6 p.m., it cools a bit, to the point that, by midnight, itrequires a sweater to be worn.

If there's a tropical storm, torrents of water are swallowed up by the red earth quickly. The calm and heat return as though nothing has happened.

Uganda's weather reminds me of the old spiritual song, "Oh Susanna," where the words say:—"It rained all day the day I left. The weather it was fine. The sun so hot, I froze to death. Susanna don't you cry. Oh Susanna."

At sunset, the shrilling of cicadas, the hammering of fruit bats, the clamor of frogs, and the deep bass voice of bullfrogs begin to tune up for their nightly orchestral performance. The smoke of native fires curls thinly about the hillsides and mingles with the mist to spill in milky pools of haze into the valleys.

The sound of Indigenous voices, softened by distance, drift on the late afternoon air. The shrill, sharp snarls, grunts and groans of the feral animals emerge in the evening hours.

Wild Africa is never far away!

The nights, in spite of the persistent undercurrent of noises, are like one would imagine Eden would be like—very different, yet peaceful.

Entebbe's luxurious white, red trimmed, Lake Victoria Hotel offers an Olympic-sized swimming pool, a manicured golf course and putting range, as well as bungalows almost hidden from view, among the trees shrouded in Flaming Bougainvillea and 'Golden Shower,' where ten giant, ancient tortoises feed.

At the Lake Victoria Hotel in Entebbe, we heard a choir singing Uganda's National Anthem, "<u>Oh Uganda, Land of Beauty,</u>" and it tells a story itself:

"Oh Uganda! May God uphold thee,

We lay our future in thy hand,

United, free,

For liberty

Together we'll always stand.

Oh Uganda! Land of freedom

Our love and labor we give,

And with neighbors all

At our country's call

In peace and friendship we'll live.

Oh Uganda! Land that feeds us

By sun and fertile soil grown.

For our own dear land,

We'll always stand,

<u>The Pearl in Africa's Crown</u>."

"FRIENDS HOLDING HANDS"—K.C. AND DERRICK, IN
BACKYARD OF OUR PROPERTY, AT COLLEGE.

SAFARI 6

There is but one road out of Entebbe—the road to bustling Kampala, the capital and largest city, and like Italy's Rome, is built on seven hills.

Formerly, on each of Kampala's hills was a Christian church. Now, the hill for a church ratio is: Christian churches—4, and Islamic mosques—3.

Thirteen miles past Entebbe, we were taken past a thicket of eucalyptus gum trees planted for anti-malarial purposes. Malaria was a major disease in the tropics and we all been inoculated against getting it, as well as swallowing daily pills.

After our previous introduction to Entebbe, we rode in a van to the capital city of 330,000 people, Kampala.

We went past the station house for the East African Railway. We traveled through a squalid East Indian bazaar to Kampala Road. This was the main street with its stately palm trees and manicured grass in the middle of four lanes of traffic, with many spaces for curb parking.

We were driven eight miles away from Kampala Road to the Nakawa District of Kampala, where the Uganda College of Commerce walled compound, with two askaris (guards), was situated. We were shown the College, then returned to Kampala Road.

Next, our driver dropped us at a Hotel, located in Kampala's ghetto district, where most of the city's crimes took place. It was very foreboding.

Our van driver said, "These accommodations have been arranged by Ronald Wood, your C.I.D.A.'s Liaison to Uganda. He has departed for his lodgings in Nairobi, Kenya. Here is a note he left for you, Bwana Jacques."

Ronald Wood's handwritten communiqué said, "This will serve as your introduction to East African living until your house on the campus is vacated. You can move in and clean it up, when advised of its vacancy by the Ugandan government representative. You may be staying at this hotel for a couple weeks or more. R.W."

Our room, at the Hotel, was on the second floor, directly above the bar, where a band played 24/7 making it impossible to get the children to sleep for any length of time. There were also tens of thousands of bats, noisily flying nightly from their nearby cave.

Our group in the hotel, was comprised of us and two other Canadian couples with small children: Edmonton's Wally and Nona Sam and their two daughters, Lara, four years and Marnie, two years-old; Arnold and Margaret Weed of Vancouver and their three year-old daughter, Penny and two year-old son, Buddy. Every adult expressed disgust at the living arrangements that had been made for us by Ron Wood.

The food, that we were served, was partly cooked and swam in three inches of grease. The meat was bright red from slabs of beef that had hung outside the hotel dining room's back door. The eggs had been collected from range-running hens. The milk was not pasteurized. The water was not chlorinated or clear. Tiny things freely floated in it. Lots of creepy crawlies abounded throughout the hotel.

Our children reacted to the food. Laura & K.C. had stomachaches. Both of the Sam kids had the runs. Weed's pair were pale and ill. It seemed everyone was taking a pill and feeling punk.

Of all of the adults, who ate very little, Arnold Weed devoured the most food. Arnold said, "Well, if the rest of you are just going to pick at your food, I'm going to eat my monies worth."

There were bugs all over the place. Cockroaches, fleas, silverfish and night crawlers abounded. Thank heavens for the wall geckos that swallowed many of them up. On entering our room, we cut off the tail of one gecko. It survived to grow a new stub.

We met with both families and discussed the matters at hand. Arnold was in favor of going back to Canada. Wally and Nona were in favour of the status quo. Sue and I, realizing there was no Canadian Embassy in Uganda, wanted to get in touch with the British Embassy and the officials at the Uganda College of Commerce. We wanted to upgrade our accommodations and food offerings, as soon as possible.

At Margaret's urging, we had to physically restrain Arnold from booking a flight out. Arnold kept repeating, "That man hanging in the square outside our hotel is an African and not a Chinese Communist killer, like the local newspaper says. Let's get out of here. It's a poisonous environment!"

Wally said, "Me and Nona and our girls are staying put till we are instructed as to when to go to our assignment in Masindi."

I telephoned Harold Baker, an Englishman, and retiring Head of Business and Distributive Education at the Uganda College of Commerce and told him of our situation.

Harold told us, "Right away, I will arrange for all three families to be moved to the Grand Hotel, a former colonial hotel of good standing, across from the luxurious Kampala International Hotel."

Harold added, "The Kampala International Hotel was formerly called the Apollo Hotel by ex-President, Milton Apollo Obote and lies in the centre of Kampala. I'll arrange it that you can all go bathe in the circular swimming pool at the K.I.H."

I wondered:—What is it Harold Baker wants from me in exchange for all these arrangements he's making for us? Will it become evident now, or when we move to the campus of the Uganda College of Commerce?

All three families voted on whether to take Baker up on his offer. The Weeds supported our decision to move to the Grand, whereas the

Sams voted to stay put at the present Hotel, because they knew they would be moving very shortly to Masindi.

That same day, Bob MacLeod, whose family of four had already been in Masindi for three years, showed up at our Hotel, to transport the Sams to their new home.

When he visited, Bob devoured all of the left over, unappetizing food at our table in the dining room of our Hotel. His stomach seemed immune to being upset from it.

Bob said, "You'll get used to this food. A little grease or oil never hurt anyone. Pass me that omelet over here, please and, yes, I'll munch into that beef sandwich, too."

I thought: This guy has an iron constitution.

Wally and Nona and their girls took off for the northeasterly town of Masindi, to join Bob and Marian MacLeod and their two pre-school children.

Bob and Wally were the science teachers at Masindi's Elementary and Junior High School. They loved golf and had talked in detail of playing many of the holes on the Masindi course that had been set up just for them. Yes, they were the only golfers.

Their master plan was: Each school morning, assign a science project to their students and then head out to play the nine-hole course in the cool of the morning. Then, after school was out, play another nine.

Later, after much practice, Wally said, "I recall nearly shooting a par round of golf. I was one shot away from it, at a tourney."

Their Indigenous caddy hunted for the balls and cleared the course of all the rocks, some of which had snakes under them. The caddy bagged the snakes in a gunnysack then speared the coarse bag till the snakes were still.

Not all the snakes were poisonous although some were and their bite would be fatal if not treated immediately. Anti-venom was accessible.

After finishing their golf game, the two Science Teachers would skin the snakes, giving the meat to the caddy and using the pelts to make things like briefcases, jackets, purses and other paraphernalia.

While we were staying at the Grand Hotel, we walked around the downtown area and noticed differences between the East Indians (originally from India and Pakistan as workers and family on the Kenya-Ugandan railway, whose offspring was born in East Africa) and the Indigenous Africans (originally from Africa's Bantu-based, Bugandan majority tribe and born in East Africa).

There were many Bugandans in Uganda speaking their native tongue, Luganda, as well as English and Swahili.

Thousands of the East Indian community paraded every Sunday stroll up-and-down Kampala Road (the main street) in their very best saris (silk wrap dresses) and tailor-made safari suits with golden jewelry, glittering bracelets and expensive Rolex watches on display for all to see.

Meanwhile, the raggedly dressed Indigenous Africans watched in awe and envy. A poorly dressed Indigenous pointed at the pompous procession and, in Swahili, said, "A summo watu." that translated into "All poisonous people."

Sue said to me, "There seems to be a hatred for the East Indian Africans. Their actions are not appreciated by the Indigenous. They are viewed as poisonous acts."

On Jan. 25, 1971 Uganda had changed hands when the, then President, Apollo Obote was attending the British Commonwealth Conference in Singapore, along with our Canadian Prime Minister, Pierre Trudeau. The revolt was an armed one.

The person now in charge within Uganda, was General Idi Amin Dada. General Amin professed that he was much friendlier to Western Civilization.

I recalled what our Liaison, Catrina Porter had said, "Amin will be a big improvement over Obote in relationships with countries like ours. Amin was taken off the streets where he'd been a bellboy at the Apollo International Hotel and trained in the army.

She had added, "According to a high-ranking, British Army commander, Amin was an athletic chap, who wasn't very smart, but professes to be very loyal to the Queen and the British Commonwealth."

After World War Two ended, Sir Winston Churchill visited Uganda often, as he continually referred to it as "the Pearl of Africa."

On numerous occasions, he offered Uganda to the Israelis. He offered it as a homeland for the Jews instead of their desired Jerusalem in Arab territory.

The Israelis had continuously turned down Churchill's offer, yet had built much of the Uganda's intra-structure of buildings and roads.

I recalled the story one British expatriate told us about their Sir Winston Churchill on one of his visits to Uganda. This one red-faced Brit, John Fox used to beam like a glow-worm when he told his:—"Winnie Story."

John Fox told of Sir Winston reviewing the Ugandan troops, in which there was a row of bare-breasted female army officers.

John said, "The emcee stated, 'Sir Winston went through the troops and was very thorough in his inspection. He was preceded by a Ugandan man who was made sure the female women were showing their best'"—as John Fox put it:—"Here comes Sir Winston and 'a titter' going through the crowd."

After telling that story, John laughed and roared so long and loud that he even wet himself. He had a raucous sense of humor.

Kampala was a city of anomalies! By day, noise reflected from the hubbub, from stores, businesses, banks, hotels, restaurants, government buildings and garages. Its streets were also crowded with trucks (lorries), cars and overfilled indigenous buses, while its bazaar hummed with trade.

The Bank of India building was unique in that all the world currency figures were displayed on its sidewall. The banks were open from 8:30 a.m. till 11 a.m. Queues were often long. It usually took 45 minutes to cash a cheque.

People took time to read the newspapers slowly (pole). The local daily was the Uganda Argus (the Voice of Africa). British, Russian, American, East Indian, Japanese and Chinese newspapers and magazines were also available from the street peddlers.

By night, Kampala was lit up with many lights used to lure people to restaurants, bars and a few private clubs. Most of the downtown streets were vacant and the locked stores and businesses had steel bars on their windows and doors. People moved about quickly in locked-door vehicles in order to be safe from kondos (robbers) and their spike belts and dead torso tosses (chucking a dead body in front of your car.)

The police station was a very busy place. The jails were full of murderers, drunks and kondos.

I hit a goat that was thrown out in front of our car by suspected kondos. In no way was I to stop. Following the instructions given by the authorities, I drove to the nearest police station and reported it and paid an imposed fine of 100 shillings.

Kampala was also a strangely beautiful place with its mosques and tropical botanical growth. It was full of people, both rich and poor. The population of 330,000 was a low figure as there were over two million in the city on the weekend. Most of these peoples arrived from rural areas for market days.

Kampala was full of zany car drivers who perform as though racing in the east African Safari Road Race. Many drivers used their car signals to tell you what to do, not what they were doing. Yes, what you should be doing with your vehicle!

Some drove their car until it ran out of petrol (gas), and then left it on the road while they went to their destination on foot. We witnessed this when we went to the drive-in movie park and on the way there, experienced many autos left on the side of the road, as well as seeing the car's occupants up a tree they had climbed to watch the cinema.

We had to be extra careful while driving within Uganda, as there were many accidents. Each year, one out of every five cars driven in Uganda was involved in a major accident resulting in death.

In Ottawa, CIDA's Catrina Porter had told us, "There was a Grande Prairie, Alberta resident, who came over with us, who happened to be looking the wrong way when he jay walked and got hit.

When we brought him home he was barely alive. Be aware, unlike Canada, vehicles in Uganda drive recklessly and on the left side of the road. We don't want you coming home in a body bag."

We had to get used to this different driving. It was a challenge to conquer.

The government's office hours were 8 a.m. till 11 a.m. It took us four weeks to buy a car due to the 'red tape.' We bought a new, duty-free, yellow Volkswagen Fastback for $3,000. Yearly insurance costs were $600.

Along with a car license, we had to buy a visa for our car. Adult people had to purchase a visa for themselves. Our kids, Laura and K.C., were included on Sue's visa.

All visas, both for you and your car, had to be shown to the border guards and stamped when we left or entered the country.

SAFARI 7

Harold Baker, an Englishman, had been the Department Head of Business and Distributive Education at the Uganda College of Commerce for the past five years. Previous to that, Baker had been the General Manager of the African Business Promotion Limited Company, for 15 years.

Harold made regular visits to see Sue and me at the Grand Hotel—updating us on the housing situation on campus as well as schooling us in—"the art of having servants in Uganda."

He told us as to what questions to ask when hiring a houseboy or girl (cook and cleaner) and a shamba boy or girl (gardener).

Since Sue would be in charge of the house on an acre lot, she, without any training, had to deal with the hiring and administration practices of dealing with African Indigenous servants.

Sue interviewed prospective servants in our room at the Grand Hotel and she settled on a twenty-year old house girl named, Ginny. Sue didn't want to employ a shamba boy or girl until we actually got on the campus.

Ginny gave Sue a list of things she would need, as well as the wage she would be willing to work for. Sue showed the agreement to Harold Baker.

When Harold looked at the Ginny's long list and the relatively high wage she was asking, he said, "Sue:—I want you to fire Ginny right away. She's taking full advantage of your inexperience and generosity."

Harold went on, "I will personally help you, Sue in the hiring of the servants in exchange for a promise from Leo, that he will take over the role of Head of the Department of Business and Distributive Education."

He added, "You, Leo will also be the acting Head of the Department of Tourism and the Department of Catering and Hospitality. Oh yes, . . . you will also be the Postmaster for the Nakawa District and Manager of the Campus duka (store)."

I looked at Harold and asked, "Do you do all this now?"

Harold said, "No, but it has to be done. I expect you to make these departments the most sought after placements by the

Indigenous. President Amin expects the Indigenous to take over the businesses and dukas (stores) of the East Indians. He also wants trained Indigenous people in tourism, catering and hospitality. In the recent past, these areas have been Asian (East Indian) dominated."

I said, "Can I have some time to discuss this situation over with my wife, Sue?"

"Okay, I'll give you ten minutes. That's all the time I have before meeting with President Amin and relaying your answer to him. It's a top priority item!"

"Surely, you must be kidding," I said, wrinkling my brow.

"No. These matters have to be dealt with quickly and that means now. You now have less than ten minutes."

Sue and I went to our bedroom to discuss the situation.

I said, "What do you think, Sue? Do you really need Harold's help with hiring your servants?"

Sue said, "Yes, I'm afraid I do, Leo. I can't seem to read these people like Harold can, but I don't want to put you in a bind concerning your work."

I said, "I'm paid to be a business administration instructor, not a multi department head, postmaster or campus store manager, but I have to access this situation. I do have upper management experience and Chartered Accounting training as well as possessing a Graduate Diploma in Educational Administration, along with my Honors Commerce Degree.

I don't want Harold Baker to report to President Amin, that I turned this offer down. God only knows what that would lead to."

Sue said, "You do what you think is right. I trust your judgment. Just don't get yourself into something you can't handle. Such a mistake would have bad effects our kids as well as us. Remember, we didn't come here as tourists."

I said, "Thanks for your input, dear. Okay, I'll tell Harold that I'll do it."

After I advised Harold Baker of my decision, he smiled and said, "I advise you to try to join the Uganda Institute of Management. In order to do that as soon as possible, you have to sit for two-hour exams in each of the following subjects: Economics, Business Management and Accounting. I will arrange for a member of the Institute to get in touch with you later today and you can take the exams tomorrow in the conference room of the Grand. Don't say no to this generous offer."

I took all the exams the next day. The Institute member, George:—a Bugandan schooled at Oxford,—had me write the exams, in his presence.

George marked them that night and informed me that night I had been successful and after giving me the Diploma in the Ugandan Institute of Management, spent a couple days filling me in on the business practices to be upheld by managers in Uganda.

He also provided me with some interesting history and background information.

The many native-born East Indians of Aga Khan's Ismali Sect were the main owners of the trading stores (dukas), and controlling most of the financial wealth of the nation. They had formed a powerful business and professional bloc in Uganda, and most of the employed indigenous African worked for them.

As a member of the Institute of Management, I met with His Royal Highness, Aga Khan, of the Ismali Islamic sect, who was a year older than I, in the penthouse suite of the Kampala International Hotel. This hotel was Kampala's highest and most modern skyscraper with its flower clock, Olympic sized swimming pool and vast central vista overlooking the city.

At that meeting, His Royal Highness, and three of us Institute Members discussed, compared and picked from application forms of Ugandan Business and Industry leaders who were interested in becoming Members in the Uganda Institute of Management, to write the exams and have the title MUIM behind their name.

Aga Khan displayed fairness and objectivity in his selections.

He said, "I am interested and supportive of Indigenous African businessmen becoming leaders in the distributive field of commerce in Uganda."

After this experience, Harold said, "I think you should join the British-run Kampala Private Club, the Kampala Rotary Club, and go on a speaking tour around the city, as well as writing a weekly column for the daily newspaper."

He added, "You have a driver and van at your disposal to go on trips with the students to every plant and industry in Uganda. Oh yes, you and your wife, Sue are invited to join our weekly, international bridge club. That way, you'll make contacts that will benefit you in the future. Just make sure you are punctual."

I followed up on these suggestions and joined all of the clubs Harold suggested.

I felt a twinge of power between my shoulders.

Sue cautioned me, "Don't you go get a big head, Leo because I won't stand for it. Just do your best! You've had high-level business experiences and possess a good education and management training:—so share it with these people. Don't let Harold's condescending attitude of:—'we're better than you are'—take hold and guide you. Be yourself and do your work for the good of your hosts, Leo."

I accepted an offer from the Rhodesian-born Editor, Tom Williams of the Uganda Argus (The Voice of Africa), to write a weekly column for African Indigenous Traders in that local daily newspaper.

The articles where to be: 500-1,000 words, written in English, with most to be translated into Lugandan and Swahili for other native weeklies. My submissions were due at the Argus office early every Monday morning. I made sure of that!

In Uganda, trade was conducted only through the MALE gender with lots of reciprocity agreements:—you scratch my back and I'll scratch yours. On buying big household items like furniture, appliances, etc., I had to accompany Sue and the sales transaction had to go through me, not her, as the seller signified his male preference.

Sue grew to love to barter, and did so through her selected Indigenous African market boy, Willie. He marketed for her, with the East Indians at their dukas over their merchandise and service. There was never a "fixed price." Sue instructed Willie as to what the bid would be, and through him, would "dicker," as to her final price.

For his good work, Willie earned a generous gratuity from Sue.

Many Indigenous Ugandans did most of the physical (grunt) work for the East African Indian Duka and Market Stall owners.

My job, as Head of the Department of Business and Distributive Education, was to train these Indigenous laborers with the skills to be able to take over the dukas from their East Indian bosses. I thought:—A fair price will be given to the previous owner.

In the daily, Argus and its weekly newspapers Amin pronounced, "The East Indian shopkeepers and businessmen must be replaced by Indigenous Ugandans. The East Indians have milked the Cow, but not Fed it!"

I was to give the Indigenous Africans Shopkeeper the tools to do the job: accounting, marketing and administrative skills.

I would have to write the books and handouts, teach and administrate a teaching staff of ten instructors, as well as manage the College's duka and Postal Station staffs.

I could teach the Indigenous Africans the tools to do the job:—Distribution (Marketing and Purchasing) and Administrative (Accounting, Personnel) skills, as well as developing them into shopkeepers. It was a challenge that would take time and effort. Time for learning new ways requires patience.

I proceeded to start to write a series of booklets based on the agricultural base and started with the first one, "Me and My Capital," and prodded the learner to examine their marketable skills and abilities, as well as how much capital they had or could raise to start a duka. "Me:"—the person. "My Capital:"—everything invested by an owner.

My second booklet was on, "The Planted Seeds of Business." It asked the learner to distinguish the items (seeds) they had to handle in order to make profit. I continued on, with, the setting up of the duka with merchandise in "Tilling the Soil." Subsequently, we went into a sales & ad approach via "Sunshine to Help Growth." We had to ask the learner to use methods that will help the items (seeds) to grow to make the more appealing to the buyer.

From there, we continued on with displaying the goods in:—"The Rain Needed to Maturity," and followed with the agricultural base with merchandise time-lines in "Weeding the Fields," to go from counting the goods. It was important for each duka owner to be in tune to, "Reaping in the Harvest" by means of Cash Analysis

Accounting, Next, was cutting expenses in "The Final Product," to be the Net Cash Profit."

Cash was used for all transactions. The reason for no Accounts Receivable or Accounts Payable was East African Socialism's extended family clause. If a trader sold his goods on credit to a buyer, that person often proved out to be a member of the seller's extended family and, as such, did not pay what he owed the seller because he or she expected the seller to forgive all their debts.

The family's male member handles every transaction. That's the way it's been done in the past and the way it was done while we were in Uganda.

The College's duka sold all school supplies; vegetables, canned goods, rationed sugar, cigarettes and the "star" seller, creams:—that lighten one's skin color.

These lightening creams, from South Africa, were in demand by the campus coeds so they could look more like white-skinned Hollywood movie stars. In some cases, these lightening creams proved to be poisonous:—accused of causing skin cancer.

One homegrown cigarette, known as "a poison stick," was sold individually, so as to meet the customer's ability to pay.

Our college duka was clerked by four alternating (shift) employees who reported to me. I was responsible for any money shortages.

I oversaw the operation by balancing the registers, counting, floating and safe guarding the cash taken in and checking the invoices and duplicate sales slips.

The internal control measures I set up, where one clerk's monetary work checking another clerk's work and vice versa. Surely, one of the two would be honest in their cash float responsibilities.

"'RED CARPET GUESTS:"—IDI AND KAY AMIN,
WELCOMED AT COLLEGE.'"

SAFARI 8

As Postmaster for the Nakawa District of Kampala, I was in charge of three part-time postal clerks who kept the post office, situated next to the college store (duka), open from eight a.m. till five p.m. daily, except Sundays.

During my time handling the responsibility for the duka, I had one incident with an Instructress, Miss Agatha Shelly, a former nun, who taught in Professional Studies.

The Head of Professional Studies, Mr. Leeky came to me and said, "I'm having trouble with Miss Shelly. She keeps saying she will not teach her English class unless she get two pounds rather than one pound of sugar from the college shop weekly. Her rationale is because she thinks she is an outstanding teacher on my staff."

There was a shortage of sugar in Uganda because President Amin had ordered most of the sugar to be exported for foreign exchange. Therefore, there was a circulated order that no one person should have more than one pound of sugar a week.

I said, "What was your reply, Mr. Leeky?"

"I told her that she was being insubordinate and will be replaced if she persists with this ridiculous demand."

I asked, "What do you expect me to do?"

"I want you to inform her of the situation concerning sugar and to back me up."

I visited Miss Shelly at her apartment and said, "Agatha:—do you realize that sugar is a commodity that operates on supply and demand?"

"Yes, but I believe my excellent teaching deserves special consideration."

I said, "Mr. Leeky appreciates your wonderful service to the students but we all have to operate on the supply and demand factors when the government has determined how much any one person can have of the commodity, sugar."

Agatha said, "Yes, but I desire it more than others do."

"Why?"

"Because I use it in my tea and in my baking."

I said, "Agatha:—Do you realize the Ugandan government has determined how much each of us is to receive of sugar since most of it is sold for foreign exchange?"

"But it's no fair. I have a sweet tooth."

I said, "Many people in Uganda have 'a sweet tooth,' Agatha, but, like you, they have to be patient and understanding concerning how much sugar can be meted out to them. That is why we have to limit everyone on how much sugar one person can buy. It has nothing to do with your meticulous service. Do you understand?"

"I do. You will inform me when and if the situation changes will you not?"

"Yes, I will Agatha and thank you for your consideration."

The only other time Agatha Shelly was up in arms is when she experienced extreme terror when she went to get in her small Dutch (Daft) car.

She came screaming over to me spouting, "A snake has wound itself around my car's clutch pedal and I am filled with fear and don't know what to do."

The snake proved out to be a poisonous Spitting Cobra and it was hit on its head with a long stick to relieve it from its lodging on the peddle.

Previous to this, I had never heard or read about a Spitting Cobra. It was pencil thin and measured six feet long

During the time I handled the responsibility of being the Postmaster for the Nakawa District and the postal shop there was one incident that needed special care.

A Ugandan Army barracks of 600 soldiers was on the property right next to the Uganda College of Commerce.

One of the Professional Studies students, Sam Omani came running to my classroom, interrupting the lesson saying, "Bwana Cuba, there's something very bad happening at your Post Office. An Army man has a gun on your clerks' head and is going to shoot him dead."

I instructed my students to stay put and work on the assignment, dropped everything and hurriedly rushed to the Post Office as quick as my legs could carry me.

A Ugandan Army Lieutenant was accusing one of my postal clerks, Ishy Patero of stealing money from his (the soldier's) letter. The Lieutenant had Ishy by the neck collar and said he wanted to shoot Ishy or be paid 25 shillings, immediately.

Out of my pocket, I quickly paid the Lieutenant the amount he was asking for. Then, we shook hands on it, ending the death threat, and he (the soldier) left.

After Ishy had settled down, I asked him, "Were you guilty of what he accused you of Ishy?"

Ishy said, "No, Bwana Cuba. I do not steal or lie. I am a Christian and follow the teachings of the Bible. God is my witness!"

Shortly after we arrived at the Uganda College of Commerce, robbers (kondos) tried to break into our house late one night.

Bonzo sounded the alarm with his barking and we telephoned the Campus Police Guards. They advised us to turn our radio up as loud as possible and to beat, with brooms, on kitchen pots, as well as the doors and near the windowsills.

Not one Campus Policeman showed up at our door. Fortunately, the dog's barking, the turned-up radio, and the pots and broom beating noise, worked.

Since the army barracks and marauding kondos were so close to the Uganda College of Commerce, Sue and I agreed to a security agreement with the Ugandan Police to have the windows of our house barred with steel and wired with alarms that would ring at their stationhouse.

In case of any trouble, the Nakawa District Police Superintendent told us, "Officers will be sent to your place as soon as possible."

This security cost us $100.00 per month.

Shortly after we had it installed, a buzzard struck a window and set off the alarm and we had 10 policemen, armed with pangas (machetes) surrounding our house.

Little did we know, that shortly after we had signed the security agreement, Amin had ordered his soldiers to confiscate all bullets for the guns of the police? Amin then had all of Kampala's 27 Police District Police Superintendents, including the man we had signed the security agreement with, executed and their bodies fed to the crocodiles at the Jinga's Owens Dam.

Our Goan neighbor, John Maris said, "My Intelligence People tell me, there were so many bodies floating in the Owens Dam that the electricity throughout that region of Uganda was affected with 'a total blackout,' for nine to ten hours."

Clearly, we had no police support! Without bullets, the police guns were of no use and left them with noise from the beat of drums, clubs and pangas to help us.

The incident reminded me of my favorite Professor who taught me Philosophy at the University of Alberta in Edmonton.

He used to challenge us Commerce students with:—Who has the most power:—the man with the gun or the man with the money?

Most of the Commerce students sided with the man with the money as he or she can always pay for protection and keep paying for such, protection to keep the man with the gun at bay. I recall some of my classmates standing on their desks yelling out.

At the time, I sided with the crafty Professor and his reasoning:—You he never "know" when the man with the gun will strike. Therefore, that element of surprise stacks the odds to favor his side. A gun, brandished with surprise, are the major elements!

I didn't account for the ultra use of "a mole" who would divulge who had the gun, or the use of robots to do "the killing," as winning elements for the man with the money.

I knew many indigenous Ugandans had been educated abroad in such prestigious places as Harvard, Yale, Oxford and Moscow. I often wondered, why all the instructors' jobs at the Uganda College of Commerce were filled by foreign (expatriate) teachers such as myself? Why weren't the educated indigenous filling these positions?

Part of the answer to that query had something to do with values expressed in research data from at East Africa's top school of learning, Makere University.

Makere's research data from 1961 to 1970, showed that many African indigenous university graduates rated their three top values as: first:—owning a $50,000 Mercedes Benz automobile; second:—having efficient East Indian clerks to kick around and pile all the work on; and third:—to have at least one big busted and big bummed, Bugandan secretary to pinch and chase around their desks.

Money grubbing, debauchery and power were their gods.

Under Amin's army rule, it didn't get any better. In fact, it was reportedly worse. His troops acted as if they thought it was 'their entitlement' to take anything of wealth or meaning from others. Amin's soldiers acted like pigs at the trough.

There was a story concerning the United States shipping a boatload of new Mercedes Benz automobiles to Uganda and when Amin charged excise taxes on the cars, The American President ordered the entire shipment to be destroyed.

That whole load of Mercedes Benz cars was set afire on the docks of Lake Vic.

Ugandan Government Statistics from 1963 till 1970, showed that nearly 100 per cent of the Indigenous Africans who had been sent abroad to study at the world's top universities and institutes, returned home without thoughts of teaching their own people, yet expected to have a much higher standard of living than everyone else.

The chain of command on the Ugandan Education Organizational Chart looked like a football on top of an old school bell.

There were so many people at the top posts with big salaries and a squeezed tight middle management (mostly made up of East Indians) with lots of peons at the bottom level, earning next to nothing in the laborers roles. The mid management level, of clerking and waiting on the above levels, was very stressful.

There were many dismembered African indigenous beggars—crippled, starving and begging at every corner in downtown Kampala.

I asked Harold, "Why are there so many beggars in Uganda?"

Harold said, "They are beggars because, in most cases, their many relatives have disfigured many of these beggars, on purpose.'

I asked, "Why?"

Harold said, "Unfortunately, it is because that way, they (the beggars) can make more money."

Yes, by begging on the street they can keep the lion away from their door.

Some beggars didn't survive when some soldier's decided to practice their target shooting on street beggars.

Our Goan Neighbor, John Mack advised when it was safe to go to the market and when it was a "Shooting of the beggars day," by Amin's soldiers, often advised us.

On such days, we stayed close to home.

SAFARI 9

The third week, I briefly met with President Idi Amin Dada.

With a broad smile, President Idi Amin Dada said, "You, Bwana Leo don't understand our extended family and East African Socialism do you?"

I replied, "I've got a good teacher in Harold Baker to learn from but I'm always interested in knowing more."

Amin, with a sly grin, then added, "Baker is white is he not? How can he possibly get inside the skin of a black man, who understands the ways of the lion?"

He added, "When a lion is injured, his mates go out and kill for him and bring him the carcass so he can dine first. The lionesses are the lion's extended family."

With that, Amin clicked his heels together and marched away. I'd been summarily dismissed and this time with a Swahili proverb.

After retirement, Harold Baker and his wife, Jean stayed on in Kampala long enough to introduce us to the British Ambassador, Richard Hale and his wife, as well as the American Assistant Ambassador Robin Kelly and his wife, June.

We met many influential East Indian businessmen, and professional men as well, some of their names are a blur to me as there were so many.

Doctor Henry Patel was a most wonderful physician and a fellow Rotarian.

Al Low was a super travel agent and advisor on safaris in and outside East Africa.

Their names stand out as our East Indian Ugandan friends. Al and his wife, Nita and family later immigrated to Canada and live in the Toronto area of Ontario.

Most of our evenings were spent in a rotating social, bridge club game at one of the couple's residences. If you didn't arrive before the stated time of 7 p.m. the door was locked with a "No Admittance" sign. Lateness was not tolerated.

Many topics, including the extended family and East African Socialism, were touched on over the social evening with the understanding, that what is said at those tables would not be discussed outside of those rooms. I became a very good listener.

The Argus newspaper was reporting ongoing disagreements between the Ugandan authorities and the London dailies. A British reporter was imprisoned as a kondo (thief) and spy when he took a telephone directory from the Kampala International Hotel. The British Ambassador intervened and the reporter was released and flown to London, and told:—"never to return." There were headlines on anti-British feelings, in the Argus.

I recall receiving a phone call from Harold on a morning after a bridge club where he said, "You were the scorekeeper for game two at bridge last night, were you not? I rechecked the tally sheet.

British Ambassador, Richard Hale should have won 50 shillings on that second hand and not the American Assistant Ambassador, Robin Kelly. What do you propose to do to correct your error?"

I replied, " I acknowledge that I was in charge of scoring game two. You say I made an error.

Okay. I will send 50 shillings over to Mr. Hale in this afternoon's mail, with my written apologies for my oversight."

I added, "Will that arrangement be satisfactory to you?"

Harold said, "Yes. I trust you will be more accurate in the future, Leo."

SAFARI 10

When we got settled in a house on the campus of the Uganda College of Commerce, we noted that the floors were rough concrete and the walls stucco. We bought large sisal mats for the floors and new furnishings for the living room and the bedrooms. After the floors were scrubbed, the rooms were swept then vacuumed. The walls were furiously scrubbed and pictures hung. We sent our Canadian refrigerator and washing machine over.

The house had a toilet, a sink and a bath but no shower. When taking a bath, I recall an army of sixty sugar ants marching into the bath, over my legs, and out the other side of the bath towards the door. When the door was closed, I noticed a gecko on the wall waiting for the sugar ants. It was a daily thing. Even in the tub, excitement ruled!

I bought an African Grey Parrot for Sue. She called him, "Siki." He was a very good conversationalist and had a great temperament. Before long, Sue had Siki talking a blue streak. His voice sounded like a human being. He was the world's gabbiest parrot.

Our house became a home that we shared with many people.

Harold was true to his word. He said, "Sue, "I have in mind for you an outstanding 51 year old Kenyan houseboy, named Lucas. He had been employed at the house of British Ambassador, Richard Hale but is being let go by them as they are going on home leave and will not require his services when they come back from London.

Do you want me to pursue him? I understand Lucas knows another Kenyan. He is Lucas's cousin, a younger man named Onyango. He could work as your shamba boy (gardener). Should I follow up on him too?"

Sue said, "Yes, Harold, by all means, please do."

"I'll get them for you at a very reasonable price. Leo will have to provide two shirts and two pairs of pants for each of them. Lucas has been clothed in a Union Jack shirt while at the Embassy. I understand that he won't be allowed to take it with him."

"That's fine. We'll provide Lucas and Onyango with two white shirts and two dark pants each," said Sue "Make the arrangements, Harold and thank you for all your troubles."

Besides cooking and cleaning, Lucas did the washing and hung it the washing on a line out back and spread some items out on the ground.

We had two Kenyan men working for us as servants. We provided shelter for them and their families. Out back of our house were the servant' house that, like ours, had of concrete floors and stucco walls. We bought sisal mats for them and helped them with furnishings for their living room and bedrooms.

Our Houseboy, Lucas and his pregnant wife, Marie had two sons: two year-old, Derrick and year-old, John.

Our Shamba-Boy (Gardener), Onyango had been out of work for a year. He and his pregnant wife, Rosa had a two-year old son, Shamil and a year-old son, Shamus.

A month later, both our servant's wives had sons born to them. There was lots of rejoicing. Everybody on our little acre was happy.

It was just two weeks after Lucas's wife Marie had her baby boy, Mathew that Lucas came to see us.

Lucas told us that they had taken their sick son to Kampala's biggest hospital, Mulago and that the medicine the doctor had sold them was not helping Mathew to get better. In fact, baby Mathew was very, very sick."

We examined and tasted the medicine and Sue found it to be only colored water.

Right away, Sue drove Marie and her baby over to an American Mission Hospital where Mathew was diagnosed to have, pneumonia.

In order to breathe, he was put in an air chamber and given strong antibiotics to fight the disease. Unfortunately, this action was too late.

Two-week old, Mathew died. What a terrible waste of a human life.

Sue said, "Marie and Lucas should have taken their child to the American Mission Hospital first. There was a caring staff there to help Mathew and he probably would have survived. One nurse from Boston had an aura to her like an angel. She was a real, caring Florence Nightingale."

We asked Lucas and Marie to come in our living room so we could express our grief and help them in any way we could. We found both of the parents very cool and appeared to be not as upset as we were over the loss of their Mathew.

Lucas summed his feelings up with, "Marie and I will have another baby. I have another wife in Kenya and can have many babies by her. East African Socialism welcomes babies to be born."

Marie said, "I am at peace with what God has done and I am willing to have another baby by Lucas, as soon as I'm up to it."

We were so astounded by their reactions that we didn't discuss the funeral arrangements for baby Mathew until another couple weeks went by.

I had received complaint from our nearest neighbor, Miss Pober, "There is a terrible stink coming from your acreage that I will not tolerate any more. I will have the authorities down on you if it's not rectified."

On examination of her claim, I discovered that baby Mathew was in a box on the top of a car that Lucas had borrowed from another

Kenyan friend. That car was parked in the back of our yard, right against the dividing hedge with Miss Pober's property. The winds had carried the emitted smell her way.

With Miss Pober, I acknowledged, "You have a legitimate 'beef,' that I will act on immediately."

Lucas explained, "We are Kenyans. We thought it would be nice to have Mathew buried in our country. Right now, we don't have the money to have a ceremony for him here. That's why his body is rotting on top of the car."

I said, "I realize you've just started working for us and may not have the monies to bury Mathew. I will pay for your son's burial here in Kampala. Talk it over with Marie and let me know your answer."

Lucas said, "I make the decisions on such matters. I accept your offer and will let you know tomorrow the amount of money I will need."

Since, I was 'snowed under' with my work, Sue offered to go, as our family representative to the church and follow the funeral procession to the graveyard where baby Mathew would be laid to rest.

At the Presbyterian Church that Lucas and Marie choose for the ceremony, the Musongu (White) Minister, whom Sue paid for his services as well as the burying of baby Mathew.

The Minister started the ceremony by putting his hand above, while giving blessings, to Onyango's live baby boy, Ollie and not above Lucas's, baby Mathew. There were whispers among the congregation but no action.

Before a full church, Sue stood up from her pew in the church and said, "Stop the ceremony. You are blessing the wrong baby." She pointed to baby Mathew, who was in Lucas's arms and said, "This is the baby boy who has died. Not the live baby, Ollie you are blessing right now."

The Minister adjusted his glasses and said, "Oops, it must be my eyesight. Let me bless the dead baby. Let me carry on."

Subsequently, Sue and many indigenous Africans sang and danced through snake-filled fields to a site where the gravedigger came out from of the jungle. He held out his palm to Sue and demanded to be paid for digging a hole in the ground for baby Mathew. He kept pushing his fist in Sue's face.

Sue said, "I've already paid Reverend Briggs for your services. If you won't dig the hole then give me the shovel. I will dig it."

Sue dug the hole and Mathew, draped in while linen, was laid in his resting place, by Lucas. The family and friends sang and danced around the grave. Hours ticked away and darkness started to show as the sun dipped. Sue realized the revelry could go on for an even longer time. She made her way back alone:—first to the church, then quickly in the car to motor home.

Driving a car in the dark is risky in Kampala as the Kondos (robbers) use spike belts and even dead bodies of humans to stop a car.

The Weeds were the only Canadian couple at the College who didn't hire servants. Arnold had promised Margaret he would pay to have new fluorescent lighting in the kitchen of their home in Vancouver with the monies they would save by not having servants. They were very frugal and opted for apartment living on campus.

At the campus, we had the four Weeds 'drop over' for dinner many times to meet our invited company. We never received a single return invitation. The four Weeds seemed to 'pop-up' at the door unannounced when someone of interest to them visited us and they hung around till the supper hour was at hand. Oh well, their fellow Canadians.

Arnold said, "After all, you have servants. Margaret has to prepare everything herself." I thought:—Margaret is a home economics graduate is she not?

I wondered:—Why were both of our servants from Kenya and not Uganda?

I asked Lucas, "Why do you and Onyango, work in Uganda and not in your home country of Kenya?"

Lucas said, "East African Socialism. In Uganda or Kenya or Tanzania, the extended family expects the one who is employed to share all their riches with them, right down to the farthest related and removed relative. So, to get away from this socialistic practice many Kenyans, like us, leave our Kenya to work here in Uganda."

After his retirement, Harold Baker and wife, Jean stayed on in Kampala long enough to introduce us to the British Ambassador,

Richard Hale and his wife, as well as the American Ambassador Robin Kelly and his wife.

We met many other influential East Indian businessmen and professional men as well. Their names were many East Indians named Patel, including a very nice doctor, Dr. Henry Patel, whom was "a prince among men." I met Dr. Henry at Rotary.

Most of our evenings were spent in a rotating social bridge club game at one of the couple's residences. If one didn't arrive before the stated time of 7 p.m. the door were locked with:—a, "No Admittance" sign. Tardiness was not tolerated.

Many topics were touched on during the social evening with the understanding that what was discussed at the tables would not be discussed outside of those rooms.

On leaving the residences where the bridge game was played, the Englishmen would swoop in on the Canadian and American wives and lay a backbreaking kiss on them. Sue said, "Harold overdoes his goodbyes."

Harold got into a tussle with fellow Englishman and Head of Professional Studies, Roger Leeky at the Uganda College of Commerce, over my availability to also instruct for Leeky in the senior accounting courses in the Accredited Accounting Association and the Chartered Secretaries Institute.

Harold said, "You have enough to do with what you are already running. The next thing Leeky will have you doing, after you instruct his beloved, professional students, is driving the 'Water for People' truck, to the quench their thirst. He's a pompous ass."

CHAPTER THREE
COMINGS AND GOINGS-ON

SAFARI 11

I lectured on "Current Management Practices" to local indigenous managers at the Public Administration Institute as well as presenting three lectures on "The ABC's Of Modern Management" to members of the United Nations Training and Advisory Centre that was lead by John Burton from England. East Indian, Joel Patel was an Economic Advisor to the Institute.

I also served, with Mr. Burton and Mr. Joel Patel, as a judge of "War Game In Five Steps:—To Design, then Build a bridge over a river in the Jungle, Near an Army Barracks; then Destroy this bridge, then Escape," played by three teams (Indigenous Africans, East Indians, Englishmen) of four men each.

The game was somewhat based on the movie, "The Bridge on the River Kwai," with a bridge to be built across a river near an army barracks, then destroyed by the best strategy, optimum timing and logistical movements of why, where and when to plant the explosives for maximum destruction, followed by the safest retreat path.

The stubborn Englishmen won the contest mainly because they would not let scare tactics of being surrounded by twenty-five Indigenous African Militia men spook them into slowing down their operation, thus favoring the Indigenous team.

General Idi Amin Dada thanked us (the judges) for our efforts. Burton and I had voted for the Englishmen's team, while Joel voted for the African Indigenous team.

Burton was so impressed with my offerings at the Public Administration Building and my participation in the war game that he came over to our campus house and offered me an 'Instructor Training Post' in the place where he'd been re-appointed, beginning January 1, 1972—Kabul, Afghanistan.

Burton, smoking a foot long cigar, said, "I'm willing to offer you five times your present salary and I assure you, the Canadian government will favor such an agreement. What's you answer. I need it right now."

I said, "Mr. Burton. I am flattered with your generous offer but will have to sadly decline it as my family and I are just getting settled. Thank you very much."

Mr. Burton smiled and said, "You and your family would be safer in Kabul than in Kampala, Leo. I hope you don't regret your decision. Good luck."

My ever-eager students at the Uganda College of Commerce were a joy to teach.

Harold Baker advised me, "You are from a colony. Therefore, you don't really understand how to teach Ugandan Indigenous boys and girls. Just watch me and learn. It will benefit you a great deal to learn the proper technique to teach Ugandan students."

I replied, "How kind of you Harold. Please show me your technique."

With a twinkle in his eye, Harold held up a shilling in his hand and to the class said, "Now, I'm going to ask you all a question and I want you to put your hands up if you know the answer. I'll pick the one of you whose hand goes up first.

If you have the right answer I will throw this shilling in the air towards you and you have to dive for it. Okay? Ready? Here's the question."

Sure enough, the students appeared more eager to spout out anything they thought was even remotely related to the question asked by Harold. The students were so keen to claim the monetary prize that they body checked each other while reaching for it.

After Harold had displayed his Behavioral Psychology teaching procedure, I thanked him for the display and gently ushered him out of the room. I thought:—How humiliating for those men and women to have to do that. It reminded me of Pavlov's salivating dog experiment.

Would B.F. Skinner have been proud of Harold's teaching method?

Still, if it works than why not try it out and see. I recalled the adage:—When in Rome do what the Romans do. Further, if the students respond positively to it, then use it, but use it sparingly as that will maximize its effectiveness. Yes, minimizing sometimes maximizes!

The following week, I tried this Classical, Behavioral Training technique out on my Business Practice class and found that they had been conditioned to it through years of its practice. Hence, I continued to use it sparingly, as I knew that an infrequent Stimulus-Response happening is the optimum way to use such a method.

Since most of my students had an agricultural background, I started by talking to them about seeding, planting, growing and reaping, in the topic:—What skills did you require to run a duka? How much money would you have to invest or attain from others like the government or the bank in order to run a duka? How can you make produce pay?

My students were willing learners and by putting it in an agricultural setting first, they were able to transfer over to the commercial setting. Enthusiasm and effort ruled the day!

SAFARI 12

My teaching schedule was completely filled instructing of several courses: Cash-Analysis Accounting (cash because there was a lack of trust), Business Law (the Laws of Uganda regarding business), Distributive Education (marketing and sales approaches in East Africa), Business English (names and definitions of business terms) and Business Management Methods (Ways to lead your business and make decisions) courses and administrating my Department's offerings and overseeing any other responsibilities related to the Uganda College of Commerce.

As well as assessing my six other Instructor's work (Two in each Department I was Head of, I managed the Nakawa District Post Office and ran the Uganda College of Commerce College Store (Duka). Furthermore, I was expected to do the payroll and performance ratings for all my Post Office and Duka employees.

My day started at 6 a.m., with a different group of three students each morning, on our veranda, to question me, while walking to the classroom.

They repeatedly said, "We want to suck out all of your knowledge from you."

I worked till noon, went home for an hour for a nap and soul food, then back to work from 1 p.m. till 6 p.m., five days a week. Most evenings were filled with giving talks. On Saturday and Sunday, I worked on my lesson plans for the upcoming week and either gave talks to business groups, attended U.C.C. or Public Administration meetings, or took a course at Makere University, to update my presentation skills.

To maintain good staff relations, I gave two weekly night Accounting lectures: one to the Professional Chartered Secretaries and one to Professional Accounting students. Mr. Leeky gave me glowing reports on his sit-in observations.

Shortly after we arrived on campus, I was asked by Mr. Twino, the Games Tutor, to act as Head Track Judge for Sports Day.

An East Indian Instructor, Ismali Core shoved his face close to mine and said, "I am going to kill you because you have taken my post as Head of the Department of General Business and Distribution. You are going to pay for this with your life."

I smiled at him and replied, "Don't be silly, Mr. Core. Think about what you are saying. I honestly mean you no harm. Let's work together."

With curled lip, he growled, "It is I who should be Head, not you."

I related this incident to Mr. Twino, who said, "I teach with Core in Economics. He's volatile and thinks he should be at a higher station here. I wouldn't take his threat too seriously. He's just jealous of you because you appear to be a management consultant deluxe. He'll get over his frustration. Trust me! Oh, I nearly forgot—our students seemed quite pleased with you and on their behalf I thank you for your interest and diligence."

The only other run-in I had with Mr. Core had been at our campus residence:—I threw Bonzo's (our dog) ball and it went through the hedge and landed in the acreage next door.

Miss Pober, our Shorthand Instructor lived there. Mr. Core was courting her. He was at her place, along with his large, well-trained German, German shepherd dog. When Bonzo entered Miss Pober's property, Mr. Core 'siced' his dog on him. A dogfight took place. Bonzo got the upper hand and had the bigger dog on his back.

Mr. Core pleaded, "Release my dog. Your mutt is hurting him."

I called Bonzo off and left the property without saying a word.

That's the last I heard from Mr. Core or Miss Pober for a while.

From the East Indian (Gossip) Pipeline:—I understand, they married, immigrated to Canada and where they later divorced.

The Chancellor of Makere University, asked me to sit in on the Thesis Committee for M.A. and PhD. students in Economics.

I served on Flint, Michigan's, Jim Mark's PhD. study, "Marketing Practices in the Dukas (Stores) around Uganda." I spent many evenings with Jim comparing notes on Uganda dukas and businesses and sharing my thoughts and lecture notes with him.

I asked Jim, "Why are you studying at Makere University?" His answer was, "Because I think it will offer me an international outlook on things and I believe it to be easier than at home in the USA because of the lack of interruptions and other things."

Unfortunately, Jim's studies were never completed at Makere. Suddenly and mysteriously, he disappeared.

At first, it was feared he'd been killed like two other Americans who had stumbled upon some unsavory practices of Amin's secret police, called the State Research Bureau.

American Assistant Ambassador Kelly advised me, that Jim was safe and sound in Nairobi, Kenya and was planning to return to America to continue his studies there.

I was asked by the Chancellor of Makere University to be the main speaker to give 'the Address' at East Africa's Commerce Graduates' Association's Annual Dinner at the Grand Hotel.

I recall Dr. Edward J. Cambers, The Dean of the Faculty of Commerce, University of Alberta and Ward Stinson, the Dean of the Faculty of Commerce, University of Saskatchewan and Matt Jergens, Professor of Business Administration and Economics from Princeton University were at the dinner.

Dr. Cambers asked me, "Could the Ugandan students you teach fare well in Edmonton in our Commerce and Master of Business Administration programs?"

I said, "Yes. They will study for 20 hours a day, if need be. They're willing."

Dr. Cambers said, "But could they measure up to our Canadian students?"

"I can't see why not. They have good intelligence and perseverance."

"Thank you, Leo. Your assessment and information is very useful to ·the University of Alberta's Faculty of Commerce and Business Administration. We are interested in expanding our international student base at the U of A."

We continued conversing about the Indigenous taking over the East Indian businesses and dukas when Dr. Cambers interrupted me and said, "Leo, you will have to excuse us right now. We are expected at the head table."

I smiled and answered, "Oh, that's okay, Ed. I'm going that way too because I'm giving the Dinner's Address on 'The Socio-Psychology of Trade' tonight."

He smiled and we chatted all the way to the head table.

Throughout my talk, the Princeton Professor Jergens kept inserting questions, "Why did the Israelis left Uganda so abruptly? "Why is there a local shortage of sugar?"

I politely evaded answering his queries and kept to the subject of my address. I didn't at first fully understand what and why he was doing that.

After I sat down, Jergens whispered, "I was just trying to unnerve you."

I answered, "For what reason?"

He smiled and said, "To see if you would bite at my trap."

I thought:—The games some people play are dangerous.

I'd hear the rumor:—The Israelis left after killing such a huge number of wildlife that they filled two Hercules aircraft. They did this as a consequence of not getting paid the huge sum of money owed them by the Ugandan government for all the building and intra-structure they had done in Kampala. The story got printed in the Uganda Argus without mentioning that the Ugandan government owed anything to the Israelis.

Further, I'd heard, via my Goan friend, John:—"Sugar was a major export and what was left in the country was being black marketed by President Amin's men."

I also lectured on "Current Management Practices" to local Indigenous African managers at the Public Administration Institute as well as giving three lectures on "The ABC's Of Modern Management" to members of the United Nations Training and Advisory Centre.

John Burton, from England, was the leader of The United Nations Training and Advisory Centre.

SAFARI 14

When we were in Ottawa, Ms. Porter had said, "You are to acquire a Rhodesian ridgeback dog to guard your house. Once you get settled in your new home at the College of Commerce, I will send you the name of the people who own it in Uganda.

When we got moved into our new digs, we learned that the returning Canadians, who had owned the animal, had taken it with them back to Canada.

An old, giant-sized Golden Labrador mix came to our door and we took him in for three weeks. We called the dog, Simba. He weighed 75 pounds.

When visiting us, Harold spotted the huge dog and said, "That is an Anglican Clergyman's dog. His servant's released it from its chain when the Minister went on a home leave to England. That way, the servant's can eat the dog's food. I believe the Reverend has returned to Kampala now. He will request that you return the dog to its rightful owner. I can take the dog to him today, as it is on my way home."

The following day, Harold brought us a smaller Golden Labrador mix for our house. We called the male animal, Bonzo. He weighed 50 pounds.

Dogs in Africa serve two purposes. They guard against robbers (kondos) and they are used as alerting humans to snakes and other dangerous things. When entering a room in a house you send the dog in first to alert you to any danger. Bonzo was also liked to chase a hard, rubber ball.

On November 5, 1971, we met two lean, young men, Hans Kraft and Ullrich Schultz from The Faculty of Forestry at the University in Gottingem, West Germany, at a downtown bar. They informed us they were in Kampala to attend the barrelhouse Jazz Band Festival and were traveling around Africa in their Volkswagen Van (Kombi) that had a steel cage inside and was piled high with tires. They explained that the steel cage is where they slept at night and when danger lurked. The tires were necessary because of the terrible roads they encountered along the way. Their goal was to visit 26 countries.

They had landed in Africa in Algeria, then on to Chad, Niger, Nigeria, Cameroon, The Congo, and now Uganda. They were both mechanically-inclined and had been on the road for 6 months.

106

They had been lost for 12 days in the Sahara desert in 120 degrees Fahrenheit heat and survived. From Uganda, they planned to go to Kenya, Tanzania, Zambia, Malawi and South Africa.

At most of the African countries they had been to so far, the border guards had taken their passports and wouldn't return these important documents to them until they had repaired all the vehicles that required mechanical attention.

We invited Hans and Ullrich to park their vehicle in our driveway and we fed them at our dining room table while they were in Kampala.

One evening, just as we were sitting down for supper, a familiar scratch was heard at the front door and Sue said, "Let the dog in, Lucas."

Bounding into the living room came Simba. Before we could react, Bonzo was on his back and the two dogs rolled and tussled all over the house while knocking down the bookshelves, cabinets and chairs. The two combatants were on their back legs, biting, snapping and snarling.

I yelled, "Grab Simba, and I'll get Bonzo." Simba lowered his head towards my voice and Bonzo's sharp teeth tore into his head and part of his ear.

I said to Hans, "You get Simba away from the dog I'm holding." With great hand strength, Hans opened Bonzo's jaws and a large snap followed as I pulled Bonzo away from Simba who was then ushered outside by Hans and Rudolph into our Volkswagen Fastback.

Sue and Arnold Weed got in the Fastback while Simba, trying to get back in our house. He rocked the vehicle so hard the car nearly went over on its side.

When arriving back at the Anglican Clergyman's place, Sue said, "Your dog came back to our place and got in a fight with another dog in our living room."

The Minister said, "Oh, it looks like my dog has a badly cut ear, but I imagine your dog is a lot worse off is he not? My dog won didn't he?"

Sue replied, "I'm surprised at your response, Reverend. No, I think your dog got the worst of it."

With that, the Man of the Cloth picked up Simba's chain and started whipping him with it. Sue grabbed his arm and stopped him beating his dog. Arnold backed an irate Sue into the car and they returned home and told their story.

The two West German fellows stayed with us for four days then proceeded on their 40,000 mile round trip, first to Kenya, then down to Cape Town and back up to Europe.

We had exchanged addresses with these two fine fellows and years later, wrote them three times, without a reply.

On January 21, 1972, we met Vic and Shannon Cummings and their two teenybopper daughters, Janet and Lynn of Prince Rupert, British Columbia, at a Kampala duka (store).

We invited them back to our place for a "good" meal and they readily accepted. They had come to Kampala from Northern Africa and were "fed up" with the food that they had endured on their safari into Africa.

Sue made sure that they had a meal fit for a king and queen. I poured the adults wine and the children soda pop. We enjoyed hearing what they had encountered on their journey, so far.

One of their stories was particularly interesting. It happened in the Sudan, where they encountered a desert and were advised by a Sudanese Officer, "To travel with a caravan of tourists in order to survive the robbers that a known to plunder and kill a family group. Hence, they joined a caravan of four family groups in order to be safe.

Shannon Cummings said, "It was like the old west in the movies, where the families went in a chuckwagon that joined other wagon's going west to seek out a new life."

Vic Cummings said, "Yes. We had a feeling that most of the time we were being watched but couldn't spot anyone during the day. It was during the night that they struck. Our campers were parked in a circle akin to the chuckwagons."

I urged, "What happened?"

Vic said, "It's better that Shannon relates what occurred that night because she was the one who was most involved."

Shannon said, "We were sleeping in our Volkswagen-Kombi van that had an air vent in the top of it. I slept right below the vent when all of a sudden this hand comes down the vent and grabs me by my right bust. I screamed bloody murder and bit the hand as hard as my jaws could come down on it and it released my boob. I woke the whole camp up and everyone's lights went on."

I said, "What happened next?"

Vic said, "The culprits ran away and I'll bet that guy who put his hand on my wife's bust has one sore hand."

Shannon piped in, "Yes. Now I brag that my bosom is so big it can't go through the top vent in a Volkswagen's Kombi-Van."

We all laughed. Shannon Cummings had experienced a close encounter of the wrong kind and made it sound humorous. She was one plucky girl!

After staying the night at our place, the Cummings headed east to arrive in Nairobi the next day. They phoned when they arrived safe and sound and that was the last communiqué we had with them.

SAFARI 15

Sue and I held a going away party for Harold and Jean Baker at our residence and invited all our Students as well as all the U.C.C. Instruction, Postal and Duka staff. The party was well attended by over 60 guests.

It seemed everyone wore his or her best party clothes.

Ten Bugandan women wore their native Kabuki dresses, with reams of material and drank their Nile beer, in 26-ounce bottles, through long straws.

The ladies from the other tribes wore mini-skirts and had their faces paled with the whitening cream that was sold at the College Store in order to make them appear more like their Hollywood idols.

The Indigenous men dressed in flashy sports clothes with draped pants. A few had Elvis Pressley sideburns and were "cool."

Most of the joyful bunch of Indigenous Africans smoked a poison stick (cigarette) that had been sold individually for a shilling at the College Shop.

The East Indian attendees flicked the ashes from their cancer sticks into their Nile Beer and let it fizz before tasting.

I asked Mr. Core, "Why do you do that?"

Mr. Core said, "To make sure it is beer and too make its taste milder."

I asked Mr. Core, "Are we now on good terms or do you still dislike me?"

Mr. Core said, "I am calmed towards you. Our students seem to like you. It's too bad you are left handed."

"Why?"

"Because that is the unholy hand one wipes his butt with."

"Well, to put your mind at rest, my friend:—I'm ambidextrous."

Mr. Core said, "You are too clever for your own good, Mr. Jacques. These are dangerous times in Uganda. I have anonymously alerted the authorities that you are teaching capitalistic ways to our students. Further, I've made The State Research Bureau aware of your treachery."

"How so? Do you care to expand on that?"

"No. You figure it out and think about your limited future here. I'll leave you with this: Om shanti, shanti, shanti"

"What does that mean?"

Mr. Core said, "May your soul rest in eternal peace."

I said, "It's terrible that you are so full of hate. God have mercy on your soul.

Then I reached for a glass of Waragi.

The local grain whiskey drink, Waragi was so strong that if a few drops of it hit the table a new hole was born. A 26-ounce bottle of Waragi sold for seventy-five cents and it was over fifty per cent alcohol.

The music was mostly fifty and sixty's fare and I recall the song, "Sugar, Sugar" kept being played over and over for the "hip" crowd.

We presented Harold with a muzee (wise man's) cane gift to show our appreciation for his wise leadership and friendship. He gave a short speech and cut the first piece of cake that Sue had made for the occasion.

Harold reminisced about his years at the College and the American and Canadian Instructors he had worked with while he was the Head of The Department of Distribution and Business. He said that one rowdy Canadian stands out in his memory.

Harold said, "This fellow was named Jack and he was from Montreal and he'd never been off the Island it sat on. And also, Jack loved Uganda's 'poison' sticks and cheap liquor, especially Waragi. He loved 50 proof Waragi!"

Harold added, "I recall when Jack and I drove to this quaint little pub in downtown Kampala. When we got back to the College's gates, we were feeling no pain. Unfortunately, there was a problem getting back into the compound.

One Askari (Guard) at the front gate wouldn't let the East Indian driver, in the car ahead of us, into the compound. Jack kept blowing his horn, but to no avail.

Jack yelled out his window, "What's the matter? Why aren't you going in?"

The East Indian answered, "The Askari:—He won't let me through."

Finally, Jack got out of his car, went to the East Indian's car, dragged the driver out and punched his lights out.

Then he got in the East Indian's car and drove it through the gates and parked it. Then he walked back and got in his car, waved at the two trembling Askaris, as he drove by them."

Harold concluded, "Do you know, after that, when I drove with Jack, the Askarais swung the gate open every time, without even being so much as asked. They also waved as we went through. I do hope Leo here will not emulate Rowdy Jack from Montreal."

The crowd politely applauded Harold's story, and he sat and smoked another poison stick.

Jean was also honored with a lovely East Indian sari and she also gave a short speech about "how much she loved Uganda."

Then, she went over and had the second piece of cake.

The rest of the evening was a mixture of dancing, drinking and conversations. Arnold Weed hung one on and really cut up a rug.

The Nation, a subsidiary weekly newspaper of the daily Uganda Argus, sent a reporter and photographer to the gala event and it appeared on the front page of their newspaper the next day, written up in the Luganda and Swahili languages.

Two pictures, with captions, appeared in the Uganda Argus, the day after. They showed Harold and Jean accepting their gifts in front of a happy crowd of partygoers.

CHAPTER FOUR
KENYA IS WORLD'S SAFARI CAPITAL

SAFARI 16

Kenya was another "pearl of a country," we spent time in as expatriate visitors. It straddles more than the equator. Its range of landscapes are truly staggered: From the north's hostile deserts, and Mt. Kenya's glaciated peaks to the dramatic depths of the Rift Valley, and the sultry shores of the Indian Ocean and Lake Victoria.

The colors of its flag are almost the same as Uganda's. Both flag's have a lot of black signifying the skin color of the majorities'; a good amount of red for the blood spilled during their existence; white is for the minority counsel and peace makers.

Kenya flag has the same amount of green as Uganda's has yellow—both signifying extremely fertile land.

Kenya's flag has a spear and shield, denoting strength via the Mau Mau Rebellion. The Ugandan flag has two crested cranes to depict the country's vast wildlife.

Lucas and Onyango wanted us to visit their relatives in Southeastern Kenya.

Before Harold Baker left Kampala for Mombassa, Kenya he had offered to us to stay at one of his cabin's on the Indian Ocean, at $175 for a week.

He said, "Each one of my cabins are side by side and has a magnificent and direct view of the Ocean. You will love it for the last week on your first school break."

Every three months, we were granted a three-week break from work. We kept Harold's offer right up top next to a visit to Nairobi, where we had ex-Medicine Hatter friends, the Simmons and the Busbys.

We were invited by them to join most of the Canadians working in Kenya to a Canadian Thanksgiving Weekend at Lake Naivasha, then on to Nairobi.

We met most of the Canadians stationed in Kenya. Clair and Gail Simmons invited us to stay with them in their Nairobi home after the joyous gathering.

Traveling from Uganda to Kenya, we got our first look at the Great Rift Valley. It was a marvelous view of the topography of the highlands and their forests and valleys.

On the way to Lake Naivasha we stayed at the Tea Kettle Hotel situated in Kenya's highlands, in Kisumu. The elder proprietors, William and Grace Cook told us many tales about how they had survived the Mau Mau terrorists.

When William found out we were interested in horses, he arranged for Laura and I to ride polo ponies, with a Swahili guide, in the highlands.

The horse I was on was a white, 14 year-old Thoroughbred-mix Stallion, named Silver while Laura rode a small pinto Anglo-Arab mare, named Paint. We were enjoying the lush countryside with its hills and dales when we came along a marked trail that the Swahili guide said we should stop at.

When we stopped I read the sign: "Lion Trail."

I asked, "Are there lions along this trail?"

He answered, "Oh yes, Bwana Cuba. Don't worry. Your horse is fast."

With that, both of us turned our charges around and rode towards the Hotel, as fast as our Cayuses could carry us.

"Hi ho, Silver, away!"

"Paint coming too, Lone Ranger."

I think Man o' War's speed record was broken that hot, sunny day.

When we got back to the Hotel, William took me aside and offered some sage advice concerning East Africa:—"Wherever you go in Kenya or Uganda, make sure you have a weapon, or something you can use as a weapon, handy."

He went on, "There are many kondos (robbers) in such developing countries. Don't display your wealth as it invites kondos to your door."

Then, he related a story of the American on safari in Kenya that hung his arm out the driver's side window only to have it hacked off by a panga (machete) because the American's wrist had a Rolex watch around it.

This happening had been widely publicized in the USA and other countries. Hence, there was a drop in Kenyan tourist numbers for quite a while.

William also noted that most kondos strike at night and "the Mau Mau terrorists" did most of their killings at night.

William said, "The black man prefers the cover of night to do his bad deeds. The indigenous doesn't have any nicer feelings of friendship towards black Americans than he does to white Americans. The indigenous would just as soon kill or rob a black American as a white American. The possessor of the money is whom he's after."

William looked me straight in the eyes and said, "I read all the East African newspapers I can. That includes the Voice of Africa, the Uganda Argus that you write your column. Here are some thoughts on your assumption of the training of the indigenous to take over the stores (dukas) from the East Indians."

He went on, "Don't expect it to happen overnight. The man that carries the sack of potatoes can't always sell it to another for a fair price. Make sure you choose an indigenous that has few favors to give to his family and extended family. The average family size in Uganda is nine. Try to select an inductee to trading with a family number of five or fewer. That way, the indigenous is under less pressure to share or forgive debts."

He went on, "Further, make sure you understand whom besides his direct family it is that he presently, or in the future, will support. Indigenous tribalism is tied to many things, and one is religion, so try to get the full picture of your future trader before you spend your time and your nation's money on training him."

I thanked William, and then related how I had observed Harold training the young recruits at the Uganda College of Commerce.

William said, "Don't be so foolish as to put down any of Harold's methods. He has been in Uganda for over 20 years and knows a great deal about the native's ways and what works and doesn't work with them. I would not classify his methods as harshly as you did. After all, a man called B.F. Skinner has a big following for Behavioral learning in America. It is a proven method and should be included in your repertoire. Listen and learn. And also, don't disregard it, Leo."

When I related how Harold had helped us hire our servants and how the Weed family had refrained from such hiring, William responded, "I think Harold gave you good advice. You two were not familiar to having servants and it's a tricky thing to understand even bits concerning East African Socialism, like the extended family."

He talked on, "Further, the indigenous African is happy when serving rather than leading. They have such a happy nature with smiles on their faces even when toting heavy loads on their heads or backs. It's like they are doing what they were born to do.

I know that sounds harsh but it's the truth because it has been that way for ages. I think you are expected to share your wealth with them through hiring them as servants."

He added, "I think you will prefer that to the alternatives of them stealing or robbing you. Think of it as an exchange of monies for work they prefer to do. In that way, you shouldn't feel any guilt for letting them serve and do the physical labor for their part of your income."

William continued, "I want to explain to you what happened when you were restrained from that fellow named after the boxer, Muhammad Ali. In East Africa, there is still vigilante justice where a person or a mob takes the law into its own hands. Since Muhammad's car had hurt your son, K.C. then you were suspected of going after Muhammad and inflict some harsh treatment on him. Therefore, you have to understand, that it why you were restrained from reaching him. Do you really understand, Leo?"

I nodded, as I continued to write down (via shorthand) all of Bill's diatribe.

William added, "You know about the practice of dead bodies or goats being thrown in front of your car do you not, Leo?"

I said, "Yes, In Kampala, I hit a goat and did not to stop my car and get out but drove to the nearest police station and reported it and be willingly to paid the sum of one hundred shillings to the officer."

William said, "I've seen white men torn from limb to limb when they get out of the car, so continue to be aware that your life depends on your reactions."

Before we left the Tea Kettle Hotel, William came over to me and gave me a hug and said, "Leo, you son of an Englishman, I think you and your family are in a precarious position and it appears that you and your wife, Sue may be smart enough to know when to ease off, relax and assess while your away from such a very dangerous post as Uganda. You've been called 'good' not 'bad' by the indigenous. Good luck to you both. Too many white martyrs have been killed or maimed in East Africa."

We drove on through the lush countryside over the Great Rift Valley as the sun bronzed the car's hood the same auto where I kept my arm inside and thought about William's counsel. I wondered:—Maybe I should ask more questions and give less oratory in the future? I think I'm going to pick some smart brains at Lake Naivasha. I understand some high-ranking Canadian veterans of East Africa are going to be present. This is a great opportunity to learn from them.

Further, I recalled a Swahili saying: "Because you want to keep your mouth shut, you will not."

At Lake Naivasha, we were treated to the sight of thousands of noisy pink flamingos rising and diving into a warm sparkling lake.

Lake Naivasha is the home of the most birds and waterfowl in the world. Pink, white, black, brown and gold colors abounded from the lake. These descendants of the dinosaurs were in "their element."

The Canadian flag was proudly unfurled and hung. There were representatives from every province in Canada at the event that attracted 44 happy people. One teenage Canadian girl walked around with a four foot, pet python around her neck. In her case, a boa is to be worn as a frill.

The Canadian Embassy in Nairobi, Kenya supplied a baked Ham and roasted turkey dinner, with all the trimmings. Our family of four passed on the meat but ate lots of vegetables and fruits.

Small talk, about what's happening locally and back home, were the main topics of conversation that took place throughout the sunny day and into the evening.

At night, the children got to sleep in the beds in the cabins while the adults slept on the floors. No one complained. It was a small price to pay for a warm happening.

Sue met a Canadian lady, Joan Hartley who had hired and fired eight servants.

Sue asked, "Where they all women? What was the problem?"

Joan said, "They all were Indigenous African women. I was scared of them. My husband, Don didn't let me go to the interviews in Ottawa. He wouldn't hire a nanny to look after our kids. Therefore, I didn't know what to expect when I came to Africa."

Sue said, "Have you hired a servant?"

Joan answered, "Yes, but I let Don give her all the orders. I'm not a person that likes to spout out instructions to others. Especially, when I'm scared of them."

Sue asked, "What do you do when Don goes to work?"

Joan said, "I lock myself in my upstairs bedroom. I'm scared to death of the Indigenous."

SAFARI 17

I sought out the guidance of the Economists from the University of Nairobi concerning my Distributive Education program, at the Uganda College of Commerce. One Official, John Wilson went over my lecture notes and gave me the thumbs up on my agricultural approach to teaching the Indigenous how to become successful duka (store) owners.

John said, "I like the way you have used the preparing for the seeding to the setting up of one's shop in an orderly fashion, then the selection of the plants that you are going to plant as being important to earning a return on investment. I also like your seeding of the plants as being the placing of the merchandise to where it will show the best for the customer.

The use of fertilizers in the form of advertising is a good way to approach it. Then the sprinkling of water with good salesmanship and word-or-mouth advertising are equally consequential.

I think the weeding out of, by trying to sell what first arrived on the shelves, by means of sales items is a point that few indigenous could understand when talking about such things as FIFO (First in, first out) being better than LIFO (Last in, first out) for goods. Musongis' (Whites') check out the due date on an item bought.

Salesmanship was introduced as bringing, "the Sunshine" in to the picture as is warms up the goods for the customer in a happy way. I think the use of cash analysis accounting, to find out how the harvest went, is an eye opener for the duka owner to know how much net profit has come from a comparing of gross earnings against incurred expenses. You have used KISS (KEEP IT SIMPLE SIMON), in a very sane manner."

I talked to as many people who would talk to me that weekend and learned a great deal about selecting the proper attitude to become a successful duka owner. There was usually a ten to one ratio in the selection process for prospective duka owners.

The East Indians, who presently owned the dukas, had shown cooperation with me, but I learned that they had little trick, like two sets of books and were masters at siphoning their monies out of Uganda, to their Swiss bank accounts.

One senior University Economic female spokesperson, under the cover of anonymity, said, "Leo. You have to understand that the

Uganda shilling is not really worth what Barclay's says it's worth. Most all of the East Indians that own dukas are moneychangers on the side."

She went on, "When the Bank gives you get seven shillings for one Canadian dollar, the moneychangers can get you anywhere from 18 to 36 shillings, for that same dollar. Hence, the East Indians prosper in the black market money exchange and are willing to take their chances on being exposed, caught and suffering the consequences. When a deal appears, as being too good to be true, beware of it, and check your perception. Distance yourself from it. Mark my words, you will be approached."

I thought:—She's given me sound advice. Nairobi is the only capital city, known to us, that has a Game Park within five miles of its downtown section. Nairobi is a bustling place with a history of white commerce as its base and with many moneymaking enterprises surrounded by a massive, tin hut slum.

There is a much different feeling in the air from Kampala. Here, in Nairobi, the feeling of British organization and Arabic marketing ways, dominate business.

The East Indian duka owners are challenged daily by the Arabic group from the coastal towns of Mombassa, Malindi and Lamu, hence are not as bold in the showing of their wealth.

One didn't venture too far from certain landmarks in case you end up in a place where extreme poverty existed. Then, kondos (robbers) strike!

With Claire and Gail Simmons as our hosts in Nairobi, we lived the high life, Nairobi-style.

We dined at top class restaurants, swam at private clubs, visited art and fashion shows, went to the Ngong Thoroughbred Horse Racetrack, and visited the Nairobi Game Park. We visited the latter many times, especially at dusk, and got to see Ostriches and Zebras, that were absent in Uganda, thanks to the tsetse fly. Most of the big cats did their hunting at dusk and night and there were many "shutter birds" awaiting the action.

Of all these happening, I mostly enjoyed going to the racetrack. The Ngong Racetrack has three entrances: One for the general public that comprises mostly of indigenous Kenyans; another for East Indian peoples; and the one we entered: for white people only.

Once inside, we were ushered to the clubhouse venue where we could view the horses in the paddock and make our selections before placing our wagers with the bookies that yipped and hyped out their odds board on each contender.

There was a lot of friendly banter among the bookies and their guests. It was a show unto itself:—a carnival-event atmosphere.

We learned, there were fewer than twenty mares on the breeding farms with only six Thoroughbred stallions in all of Kenya.

Therefore, many of the runners were closely related and a lot of inbreeding took place.

Even, full brothers and sisters were mated.

Still, that didn't deter the enthusiasm of the joyous crowd as they milled about and made their wagers. Many a musongu (white), male enthusiast was dressed in top hats and tails, while their women wore lovely dresses and big, plumed bonnets.

The races were run in true British style over hills and dales on a mile and-a-half course, with the runners barely visible, at certain stages of the race. Tally-ho runners!

Lots of liquor was consumed, as one tried to follow the race through the provided binoculars.

Friendly waging rivalries took place where one person in the crowd would ask the rest to pool all resources so that he could wager on a "sure-thing."

SAFARI 18

The Swahili "golden age" emerged in East Africa between 1,000 and 1,500 A.D., when major Swahili trading ports such as Mombassa, Malindi and Lamu emerged as a distinctive commercial culture on the shore of a very big body of water, the Indian Ocean.

Our family was fortunate to often travel to Kenya, the country of our servant's (Lucas and Onyango) relatives. Lucas and Onyango were both of the minority Luo tribe and grew up near the Kenyan/ Ugandan border.

Our second trip to Kenya, we again visited our Canadian friend's, Clare and Gail Simmons and family in the capital and largest city, Nairobi (Maasi phrase for "the place of cool water.") Our hometown, Calgary is Gaelic for "cool running water."

It seemed like a good idea. Still, it would be imposing on the Simmon's. We knew the Simmons from Medicine Hat where Clare and I had taught. We were all members in playing couple's bridge club that met weekly.

I had taken courses with Clare when he was getting his Master's degree in Vocational Education at the University of Alberta. Clare had been seconded from Edmonton's Northern Institute of Technology to the Kenya government; to use his civil engineering and vocational education expertise needed in order to build polytechnic institutes for them.

Clare and another Canadian, Dr. Bob Busby (PHD, Oregon State College) had been engaged in this intricate work of plan drafting Polytechnic Institutes of Technology for the government of Kenya.

The Canadian government had donated millions of dollars towards this venture. It was billed as:—"An exciting step into the next century for Kenya." There was a dire need for tradesmen and technicians in East Africa.

Due to time commitments, we decided to take the more direct route from Uganda to Kenya via the Tororo road.

Just past the town of Tororo, we had to stop at the border entry post, where the guards directed us to go into the building to show our passports, as well as the passport for our car.

In East Africa, your car has a separate passport. Your children are included on your wife's passport.

The post's parking lot was only 10 yards from the road, with two buildings 200 yards from the parking lot. Sue and I left the children in the car, with the doors locked and walked towards the largest building.

Outside the building, there was a crowd of people, made up mostly of women, holding small babies. I'd estimated, thirty or forty of these women and a few men.

When we got inside the dreary building, a guard ushered me to the front of a long line, while Sue stayed at the back, near the front door.

I went up to the counter and the Indigenous Clerk on duty said, "How can I help you Bwana Cuba?" I held out my passport, as I pointed and said, "My wife, over there, and I are traveling to Nairobi, Kenya and have come to have our passports stamped."

The Clerk quickly grabbed the passports.

Then, he stepped back, turned around and lifted his right leg high in the air and, "Kpow! Whack! Kpow!" The cabinets in the room swayed to and fro.

He had kicked something, or was it somebody, against the wall behind him? I heard a gasping and yowling then saw, a young Indigenous man dragged, by his feet, out of the building and into the courtyard between the two structures. One of his sandals had come off, as he was towed outside.

I viewed the goings on from a large window in the main building.

Outside, in the courtyard, the man's other sandal flopped to the side.

Two policemen, brandishing long, bullwhips, mercilessly sliced into the man's face and body—as he was yelling "Idi! Idi! EEK! Idi! Idi! EEK! Idi!

These bullwhips weapons, expertly handled, savagely cut, beat and hammered into the man's torso. The whips crackled in the air:—WHACK! WHACK! WHACK!

Putrid smells sought out my nose. Human feces.

Like a misty body, the crowd moved closer, closer and closer. I started to breathe deeply, almost pant. My head was pounding. My ears:—alert to every sound. My teeth chattered and clicked. My stomach churned and morning breakfast nearly came up. My tongue tasted funny:—bits of iron.

First, all the man's clothes were gone. The smell of blood and raw meat permeated the air. Body parts of the man flew in all directions. It was horrid!

An ear.

An eye.

A hand.

A forearm.

The bowels.

Everything imaginable.

It was extremely noxious!

Dreadful!

Explicit inhumanity to a fellow Human! The hair on the nape of my neck was stiff like a wire brush. My hair started itching. I kept closing, then opening my eyes.

From the building's window, I noted the ear-to-ear smiles on the lips of the African Indigenous women, rocking their babies to and fro.

Why would they enjoy this, this . . . kind of butchery?

Sue was trapped in a corner of the room, behind piles of people packed in like sardines. She was near the front door, yet couldn't exit.

I thought: What a terrible way to die! Get hold of yourself big guy.

Just then, "the kicking clerk" grabbed me by the arm and said, "Who did you say you were with?"

"Embassy! Embassy! Canadian Embassy," came from my quivering lips.

"Oh, then Bwana Cuba, please get your dear wife and come with me to the other building over here so I can be of service to you properly. Just follow me, sir."

This juxtaposition of savaging against "their own" and this civility to expatriates was very revealing. It was the clerk's matter-of-fact attitude, contrasting the cruelty and inhumanity towards the victim. It was eerie! It was an atrocity!

Pointing to the now prone, dying man as his squeals faded to be last breathes, I quietly asked, "What did he do?"

"Oh, he's 'a very bad man.' He stole a chicken. Now, let's process your passports, Bwana Cuba. No more talk of that bad, bad man."

"Could I have paid for his crime and his life spared?"

"No. Not at all. The bad, bad man has to pay with his life. He:—wrong tribe."

The three passports were stamped and we were quickly ushered, by a hand in the middle of my back, to the door by the wide-smiling clerk as he said, "Give my best to your Embassy, Bwana Cuba and have a nice and safe journey."

I nodded and grabbed Sue's hand as we walked briskly to our car and tapped on the window for Laura to open the door.

We got in our car and said nothing.

Not a thing! We were stunned, shocked and silent.

Laura asked, "What was all that terrible shrieking all about?"

We were tight-lipped. My throat was as dry as the desert sand and my neck throbbed.

The images of that poor man blurred before my eyeballs.

Sue didn't talk either. I looked at her and there were tears in her eyes.

We remained silent for a long, long time.

We absorbed the stunning beauty of the Great Rift Valley, without uttering a word.

We were quiet ones, occupying the front seats of our Yellow fastback.

Everything was quiet, except for the humming of the motor and Laura's continuous questioning, "What happened back there?"

Still, not a word passed from our lips.

Finally, as we cleared the Great Rift Valley escarpment and started to descend, I said, "Back there, we witnessed a terrible killing of a human being and I didn't, I mean couldn't, do anything to stop it. We felt sick to our stomach.

"Are you going to report it at the next police station, dad?"

"I don't think so dear. The police were present at the border and they seemed to have been okay with the actions. As a matter of fact, both of the men who killed the poor victim wore a policeman's uniform."

More than once during my life, when I think of the terror of that incident, I recall what had come first to my mind: Could I have saved the man? Was it possible? What were the odds? How could I save Sue and the kids if the guards decided we were 'bad'?

Sue also had second thoughts and feelings about that day at the border post.

She said, "What was wrong with those women? They were smiling while that human being was beaten to death. How can they treat a fellow countryman that way? Where is their sense of justice? It seems like vigilante justice prevails here. It's poisonous!"

SAFARI 19

As a country, Kenya seemed more stable than Uganda. When Kenya got its freedom from British colonialism in 1963, the country's first President was Jomo Kenyatta.

Kenyatta had been suspected to be a 1950's 'Mau Mau' terrorist leader, taken as a prisoner-of-war during that uprising, but now was revered by his people and admired:—even by his former foes. He'd even taken on the name of his beloved country.

I met him at the East African Institute of Management Conference, held at the University of Nairobi. President Kenyatta was in his late 70's—a thin, frail man with a white beard and a wobbly cane in his left hand. In his other hand, he held a tasseled stick, given him by the people of Kenya, as a token of their esteem for his being a muzee—"a revered, old person."

Being "an old person," was an honor in East Africa, where life expectancy was in the late 40's.

Jomo's face was glowing as looked me in the eyes; spoke softly with his greeting while carrying his little, muzee stick that he kept gently flapping on his thigh.

I thought: His words are golden to all. He is loved like a Saint! I'll bet even President Idi Amin listens to him and the odd time tones down his (Amin's) viscous plans towards other human beings. Jomo seems good for East Africa.

Sue said, "Jomo is like Solomon—wise and a pearl! Idi Amin is like the devil—evil like poison!"

Clare and Gail Simmons had a raucous social lifestyle while in Kenya.

Gail said, "Since being assigned by C.I.D.A. to Nairobi, Kenya, this past year, we have entertained 320 times in our home and another 25 times at our Private Club."

Gail added, "Thank heavens for the houseboy. He's a great cook. I'm worn out being hospitable and gracious. Our two girls Margo (13 yrs.) and Jody (10 yrs.) are enrolled in private Nairobi boarding school."

She went on, "Joan Busby (Bob's wife) and I are enrolled in a four-year bachelor of education degree course of study with the Kenya-based wing of San Diego International University."

Gail added, "We spend a lot of time in the Game Parks, like the Nairobi Game Park (eight miles from Nairobi's city limits), the Masai Mara Game Park (bordering Tanzania's famous, Serengeti Plains), Tsavo Game Park (60 miles southeast of Nairobi) and others, even further away. Our teacher-student ratio is 1 to 4."

It seemed like these expensive courses were held within nature's flora and fauna and very enlightening for an expatriate. The low ratio should be great for learning.

Shortly after we arrived, Clare told us that they had again arranged for all the adults to go to the Ngong horse racecourse, as he said, "to bet on the ponies."

One Kenyan stud was named, 'Simba's Sultan,' and I bet on his pitch-black son, Aga's Sultan in the Kenya Derby. I was rewarded with a twenty to one payout.

Clare put two hundred shillings on Simba's Sultan nose and was the big winner in our group.

He said, "Thanks for the tip, Leo. I knew you would bring me the winner and the luck that goes with it."

That evening, on Clare's nickel, we all went to the Kenya Club and dined and danced the night away. Everybody loves a winner and the swank celebration that follows.

Right after the race, Sue had made arrangements with a Kenyan artist to paint an oil picture of the start of the Derby. It was delivered to the Simmons's place the morning after the race and Sue presented it to me.

Even though, now curling up, it still hangs in the hallway of our house, today.

That same morning, Clare said, "Leo. Would you like to go golfing with Bob and me and some buddies at our club's exclusive golf course."

I agreed to his offer and Clare provided me with clubs and shoes for the course.

I thought: Clare is one great guy. He is so organized and thoughtful.

Early the next morning, after a light breakfast, we got into Clare's low-slung car, a Citroen (a stylish French auto that provides a smooth ride over bumps) and off to golfing we went. At least that is where I thought we were going.

We went into this spread out, motel-like building nestled in the eucalyptus trees and met up with Dr. Bob Busby and two other fellows whose names I recall as Jack and the other, Joe. Clare said both Jack and Jim were Vocational Education Teachers from the University of Alberta that were on assignment in Kenya.

After introductions, I said, "Well, are we all ready for a good stroll on the golf course?"

They all laughed.

I turned to Clare and said, "What's up?" Then I spied what was up.

A swaggering, loudly dressed 30-ish African Indigenous man and five brightly dressed East African ladies-of-the-night strolled up.

There was a pairing off and the other duos disappeared behind curtains.

Dumbfounded, I was staring into the eyes of a 20-ish lithe, light-brown skinned Kenya woman.

One of my favorite songs, 'Sugar' echoed through the room and she said, "My name's Candy. Wanta dance, Bwana Cuba?"

I replied, "No, thank you. I . . . I'm going golfing."

"Not right now. You're dancing with me."

She grabbed my hands and flung them around her waist and wiggled her hips from side to side. I stood still, dropped my hands to my side then lightly pushed her away.

I said, "I'm sorry but I'm a happily married man . . . . What do you usually get paid?"

A scowling pimp said, "Two hundred, fifty shillings (about 36 dollars.) You pay me."

I handed the money to Candy and said, "Here, you take it and give him only a small part."

"Thank you, Bwana Cuba. It will help me feed my children."

I grabbed the Pimp by the collar and said, "Where has Bwana Simmons gone? Tell me or you'll be staring at the ceiling."

"Oh he's in room 16 right now. I can get him for you, Bwana Cuba."

I said, "Tell him that I'm mad as hell at him."

Thirty or forty minutes later, Clare came bounding into the room.

Clare said, "You're a strange one, Leo. That Candy's one, 'Hot Babe!' She's your, 'Jungle-Bunny!' What's wrong with you, man? This beats golfing any day."

I said, "If you'd been up front with me, Clare, I would have declined your offer and spent time with my family. Your being two-faced really upsets me. Will I have to call a cab to go back to your place, or are you all finished here?"

Clare said, "I'm finished. Don't say anything to Gail. We're on the road to parting ways anyhow and I don't want to give her any edge. She and her high-priced professor make sultry music out in the flora. The jungle whispers!"

I thought: So the Simmons are in for a split. Even though Laura gets along well with Margo, she won't be going to her place in Nairobi, on any of her school breaks.

When we arrived back to Simmons's, I asked Sue, "Do you want to go to the Coast and stay at Baker's Cabins in Mombassa for a few days? I give my lecture at 10 a.m. and can arrange to miss the last few lectures at the University tomorrow so we can take a few days off before heading back home."

With regards to Clare and Gail, I thought of the Swahili proverb that says:—"Abuses are the result of seeing one another too often."

Sue agreed, provided, I make sure it was okay with the Kampala Registrar of the Institute of Management, who had said to me:—"I want you to put forth your core ideas of 'How the Indigenous Can Improve as a Shopkeeper,' and make contacts."

The talk was based on how being a farmer in agriculture and being a shopkeeper in business are similar, yet different. The emphasis of the talk was to be on the similarities rather than the differences. I had a "Follow-up Talk" lined up to harp on the differences.

That evening, we saw a humorous, British play. The next morning, after breakfast, I headed for the University of Nairobi; gave my lectures; then back to Simmons, to pack up my family, thank Clare and Gail for their generosity and drive to the Indian Ocean's coastal port, Mombassa.

SAFARI 20

Upon arriving at Baker's Cabins, we found Harold Baker, without his "rug" off, running around with a panga (machete).

He said, "I'm getting a wild pig supper and you're invited. Now, let me get that wild pig! You go relax with Jean."

Jean Baker showed us to our quarters, a small cabin facing the Indian Ocean. There were curtains for doors and two spider monkeys drove Sue to distraction by hanging down, swinging in and taking anything they could get their hands on.

Sue went into Jean's kitchen and helped her with the boiling of the crabs.

As the remainder of our family laid down to rest, a leopard came by the doorway, looked in, batted his eyes then took off. Then, we heard Harold bashing and banging a tin pan, yelling, "Supper will be served in one-hour's time. Roast pig tonight! Boiled crabs tonight!"

That Harold . . . he never grew up! Here he was a 51 years old and acting like a schoolboy. You could tell he loved East Africa, especially Kenya.

We had a delightful supper, but Sue complained, "That roast pig tasted so alive. I didn't feel well after I ate it. I loved the boiled crab and should of only had it."

I said, "Why don't you take some 'Kaopectate' medicine for your stomach? We did bring it along didn't we?" Sue had brought along some other stomach medicine.

Before retiring, I asked Harold, "Is there anything you can tell us about going into the Ocean tomorrow morning?"

"Just don't go past the reef. That's where all the Great White Sharks are. Outside of that, there's nothing to fear but fear itself. Trust me!"

Our twelve-year old daughter, Laura asked, "Why aren't there more people on the beach?"

Harold said, "Oh, the Indigenous and East Indians figure they don't need a tan. It's only us crazy musonges' (whites') who desire to change the color of our skin by roasting in the sun."

Laura said, "We have with us some 'Bag balm' (a Lanolin based cream used on cow's udders to prevent burning and overheating) to keep the sun's rays under control." Harold said, "Doesn't it wash off in the water?" Sue answered, "No. It stays on until you wipe it off with a towel or rag."

Next morning, the miles and miles of white sandy beach, beckoned like the calling of an enchanted island. Our family of four went to the deserted beach and enjoyed snorkeling among the colorful fish and coral in the warm waters of the Indian Ocean. The temperature was eighty-nine degrees above on the Fahrenheit scale. For hours, we all splashed, swam and snorkeled in the azure blue water that was like a luke-warm bathtub. Sue watched after K.C., as he made sand castles and pretended to lower the moat for the caravan to enter.

Sue said, "It's a lot warmer than we're used to. I think I'll go get a soda drink and start preparing lunch on the beach." Three-year old KC went with Sue.

Laura and I stayed in the water and concentrated on brightly colored fish, large red-necked turtles and multi-colored star-fish that lost their hue, when beached. KC was enthralled by the star-fish and came back into the water. I stayed within 10 yards of him at all times.

Sue chirped, "Don't you think it's about time you all came in?"

Laura was first, of us three, to reach the shore, while KC and I stayed to collect more seashells and clams.

We were about forty yards from shore, in about two feet of water, when something strange happened. KC had his pail full of seashells and clams.

Out of the corner of my eye, I saw something moving towards him in rapidly. It appeared to be a large clump of purple seaweed that looked like an armed battleship from days of yore.

I spun my heels in and faced it. It seemed to pick up speed. I thought: There must be changing winds direction.

At first, it was 60 yards away, then 40, and then 30. I wet my finger and raised it in the air. No:—There's no gusting wind. "Timesawastin!"

"KC! GO TO YOUR MOTHER, IMMEDIATELY! LEAVE YOUR PAIL AND GO. RIGHT NOW! GO, SON! QUICKLY GO!"

I intercepted the monster sea craft before it reached KC.

Tentacles shot out and around my left leg and up my back. The long arms of the beast quickly wrapped themselves around my thigh and calf, scorching my upper back. It dug in.

Our tropical heaven had turned to horror!

There was a high-pitched gurgling, sucking sound. My leg, limp! Pain shot up! Oh, my head! "Eek!" It ravaged my entire body. I thought I had a high tolerance for pain. This must be like sitting in a turned on Electric Chair!

I bent down, reaching with my left hand, dug my nails into the foamy, bubble top; grabbed into the bubbly and weedy tissue of "The

Thing," and, with all my strength, I ripped it off my torso and tossed it out to sea. Instantaneously, there was an explosion of loud popping. It thrashed its legs violently and aimlessly in the sunlight.

I yelled, "There! It's gone! I'm coming in!"

With clenched teeth, I pivoted on my right leg and dragged myself towards shore. A whimpering KC was already in Sue's arms—being toweled down.

Poor little guy! He was scared to death!

I was becoming more and more dazed. Distantly, I heard Sue:—"Get out of the water! You're all red! Get out! You look terrible!"

I thought:—You can! You can! With the grace of God, you can be triumphant in tougher times than this. Keep moving! Mobility. Do it! Do it now! Now!

On the beach, I collapsed. Sue threw a beach towel over me, quickly covering the wavy red welts on my injured leg and shoulder blades.

While putting an ice pack, wrapped in a towel on my left leg, Sue said, "I don't know what to put on your injury, Dear. How are you feeling? Can you walk any distance at all, Leo?"

"I'm rocky. If you mean—cabin? The answer is no. No can do!"

Sue replied, "I'll have Laura go get Harold and Jean. They'll know what to do. Hang in there, Dear? I love you! I love you!"

I nodded and then heard Laura's feet scampering, "off-and-running" for help.

I felt woozy, then blacked out. Suddenly, Harold's blurry image appeared.

"Hi. 'Gotta-a-bit-of-a' problem, Chum? We'll look after you, Ol' Boy. Stiff upper lip."

I tried to gulp in air. My head was throbbing, whirling! Deep darkness! Struggled! Wanted to stay awake! Wanted to . . . .

As I went in-and-out of consciousness, Harold ripped off the towel.

I think I heard him say, " Whata hell-ova sight!"

Then, I did hear him say, "You've run into something I haven't seen in these waters for years."

He lifted my head, tilted it back, gave me blue pills with some water, most of which dribbled down my face and neck, and said, "These are strong, anti-venom pills for the poison in your system. Just keep calm. Relax. You've got to stay calm. Don't move at all. Rest."

"What? What was . . . ? What was that thing?"

"Oh, that was a Portuguese Man of War. It's a colony of organisms that, when it bites, shoots a poison into your body that is eighty per cent as lethal as a Hooded Cobra Snake. They are real nasty things."

"Is there an anti-venom for it? 'Yikes,' this pain is increasing. It's really severe now!"

"Yes. I've already given you all the serum I've got. Jean's gone to the Ranger Station, down south, to get more. She and Ranger Burns should be here shortly. You just rest. Don't get worked up. You're in safe hands. You're a fortunate young man to have this encounter so close to shore. Very fortunate! Be calm. The pain will eventually subside."

"How so? Could you tell me, again?"

My heart was throbbing. Now, I could barely breathe. I was again, in-and-out of the light again. Awake! Pain! No! Blackness? Yes, I'm awake! Increased pain!

Harold said, "Now, as I was saying, if you had been any further out it would have been curtains for you, my friend. Do you understand that?"

"Yes, but what are they? When I hear Man o' War I think the greatest racehorse of . . ." I slipped out of consciousness once more.

Harold said, "My friend, I'll have your Sue explain what a Portuguese Man of War is. I understand that Jean and Burns are on their way here. I'm going back to my office. Don't worry. You're going to be okay. You're as strong as an ox. Cheerio!"

I looked up at Sue and said, "Don't worry about me, dear. You heard what Harold said. I'm lucky as a leprechaun and strong as an ox. Nothing can beat that combo? Right?"

"You surely have someone watching over you, Leo. Just don't think too much right now. Lie still. Don't mix the poison with your blood. Stay positive. You're going to be okay."

Ranger Burns came with another man. They rolled me onto a stretcher, put warm towels over my body, and gave me more pills to gurgle down.

Then, they took me to a waiting ambulance and I was off to the Health Clinic. It was there I spent the next three days. Every time I woke up, a pleasant nurse was giving me more pills and telling me: "Hush! Go back to sleep. You need your sleep, Bwana Cuba."

Finally, I felt better. I could breathe easier than I had for the past couple or so.

I thought:—I'm still, alive. Thank you, God. Some Plastic Surgeon or Dermatologist is going to get rich on me.

My shoulders and left leg was covered with wavy, red welts. I still had some pain, but nothing like before. My torso was not as uncomfortable, but real itchy.

Calamine lotion was the answer. I was also given a cream that had lots of Vitamin E.

Sue said, "Great! You're going to be able to get up and walk around. Just take your time, Dear. You look like you're recovered from those nasty bites from that awful thing. The nurse has given me a Med-Pak for you."

I got up, kissed my wife, hugged my children and shook hands with the nurse and doctor. Tottering on two unsteady legs, I sat down on the bed. Then, I got up and walked out of the room and down the hall and back. I was mobile again. Praise the Lord!

SAFARI 21

We stayed that night in Baker's cabins.

Early, next morning, Harold came over with his 20-year old daughter, Patty, who'd been born in Uganda.

Harold said, "Well, 'Old Boy,' you look ship-shape enough to see we two off on an ocean-liner today. Are you and Sue game for it?"

"What? You mean both Jean and you are leaving Mombassa? Why?"

"I've been offered a lucrative job in my home town in England, and Patty and I are going aboard and Ocean-Liner to Australia, to spend some time, then England. Jean will stay a here for about a month, then go directly to England."

"Congratulations to you. You've earned it! Well done! I'm happy for you, Harold. When did you say you and Patty leave?"

"At 13 bells, Old Chum. They'll come pick us all up in a small boat and take us out to beyond the reef where the liner awaits. You and Sue can come out with us. Then, come back, as we sail off. What do you say?"

"Well, I'd love to go see you off, Harold. What about you Honey?"

"No, I'd rather not. I have to stay behind for KC. He's still not sleeping well. You go ahead, Leo. Why don't you take Laura with you? She's never seen an ocean—liner. Ask her if she'd like to go."

I asked Laura. She was thrilled to go.

It would be something special and out of the ordinary that any twelve-year old would love to experience—I least thought so.

The ocean was angry that afternoon! Our tiny craft bucked and bobbed in the breaking waves. My stomach felt 'woozy' like riding a rodeo Brahma Bull.

The entire trip out, Laura had a Cheshire-Cat smile, stamped on her face. Our darling daughter must have an iron stomach. She makes her "old man" appear to be a frightened "landlubber." She may be right. I didn't feel healthy.

We reached the big, rolling Ocean-Liner and marveled at its seemingly limitless size and beauty. We went up the ladder and onto the ship. It was an exhilarating experience, like something one did that could turn thrilling beyond terrific. What wonder!

While we stood there, my thoughts wandered back:—We had previously spent a week at Baker's Cabins. Maybe, this time, as a side trip, we should go up the coast to the Arabian-styled town of Lamu. One tires of lounging on an "Eden-like" beach setting all day long.

Suddenly, Harold was tugging at my sleeve and said, "Well, Leo. On this card is our new address in England. Please write us in a month or more."

He extended his hand to me. I gladly latched onto it and gave it a hefty shake.

I said, "All the best to you and Jean in your new posting. All the best to you and your daughter, Patty on your trip to Australia."

I then turned to Patty and shook her hand. Out of the side of my eye, I saw Harold grab Laura and lay a big, passionate kiss on her while bending her back. Our surprised, "tee-ny-bopper" daughter yelped, "Ouch. That hurts!"

I rescued her and hugged her. Harold and Patty were gone. Disappeared into the bowels of the ship.

The deckhand stopped me in my traces as I chased after them in the direction I thought they had gone.

He said, "Sir, you have to go now. The engines are fired up and we have to hit the seas when they're revving. You have to leave right away."

He led us to the swaying ladder, rocking to-and-fro and, "plunk," we were in the small boat again.

I hugged Laura close and said, "I'm so sorry, dear. I'm so, sorry! I just don't understand why he did that."

She was crying softly on my shoulder as the angry sea rocked us with its rolling waves, the rest of the way to shore.

During our return voyage, the only things that were lost were a friendship and an English address that I tossed into the Indian Ocean.

I still don't understand:—why a 52 year-old man would embrace and swoon-kiss a 12 year-old girl.

Harold was a classless human! I 'shoulda' dropped him. I 'woulda,' and I 'could have.'

My stomach churned more from that memory more than our little boat being bounced and bashed by the briny.

Back on shore, Sue had been receiving African beauty tips from Harold's wife, Jean, as KC played with his sandcastles.

I heard Jean say, "Now, Sue dear, do not forget to put a cream like 'Noxzema' on your skin, after being in the sun for any length of time."

Sue said to me, "Jean has been so wonderful for letting me in on her tropical beauty secrets. She's so vibrant and young! She's a lovely woman."

"That's nice, Sue. She has her challenges."

"What do you mean by that, Leo?"

"Oh, nothing, I'm happy, that you're happy."

"I forgot to ask you how your trip was on that stormy sea, Dear?"

"We survived. The only casualty was an address and it's lost forever."

"What? Oh, you mean you're not going to see the Royal Caledonia Ocean-Liner again. Well, we've got to finish off packing if we're going to make it to Malindi by check in time. I booked us into a classy German hotel, there."

We bade fond goodbyes to darling, Jean, drove to Malindi, checked into our hotel, then off to downtown in this Swahili settlement that dated back to the 14th century.

SAFARI 22

Malindi (once called Melinde) had once rivaled Mombassa for dominance, as a port-of-call, in this part of East Africa. Malindi had traditionally been a port city for foreign powers. In 1414, the fleet of the Chinese explorer, Zhueng He, visited the town. The Ruler of Malindi sent a personal envoy, with a giraffe, as a present to China.

In 1498, the Portuguese explorer, Vasco da Gama met Malindi authorities, to sign a trade agreement and hire a guide, for the voyage to India. Da Gama had erected a coral pillar in Malindi, which stands to this day, though there have been calls by conservationists to maintain it, lest it fall.

In 1499, the Portuguese established Malindi, as a resting stop on the way to-and—from India. A church, dating back to this date, still stands.

Malindi is, a popular tourist attraction for many middle and upper class Kenyans, as well as some international tourists. The Germans built luxury hotels, so that the staff's of German industries and business places, could have bonus holidays, in stunning settings.

These luxury hotels, are situated in an area called Juma Mosque and are designed in the form of palaces on the beach, stretching out into the Indian Ocean. They are designed mainly with, "an Arabian touch."

Our year-old hotel was set in, what one would imagine Ali Baba would have lived in. The rooms were full of Turkish tassels, rugs and pillows. The floors were charcoal black shale rock with rose imprints. The walls were painted in bright yellows and greens with light brown trimmings and the bathroom were a marbled grey with ivory trimmings. The view from our balcony was stunning, as it overlooked the inlet from the Ocean.

When KC was snuggled in bed and Laura was reading a book, Sue and I went down the modern elevator to the dance hall that opened out into the Ocean.

We danced while the thunderous waves splashed against the sides of the wall. Whirling water splashed on the grey-shale dance floor.

A seven-piece band, named, "The Modernists," played popular music, for hours and hours. We danced and danced the night away.

It was heaven, holding Sue in my arms. What a lucky guy I was. She's sweet as "a honey-bee's syrup."

All of a sudden, it was way past midnight. The aroma of seafood permeated the air that also reeked of changing texture from the concrete floor. There was a mysterious crackle of the palm trees, being jostled by the wind. Cinderella and I had to retire.

The next morning, we checked out of our hotel, ate breakfast, parked our car and went shopping. The fabric cloth, Kitange is a colorfully designed, cotton garment from various Far-East countries. The most expensive ones are from the former Dutch colonies and they are plentiful on the Kenyan coast. They cost a lot more than the ones we had previously discovered in East Africa. They were worth it!

The African Safari suits for men were handmade, with great care. The entire family enjoyed shopping at the stores where the merchandise, hung in the shop doorways. Sue bought yards and yards of Katangese material, with visions of making different items from it.

Sue is a good seamstress and loves to make things for the family.

Shopping in Malindi was a dream come true for her.

173

In respect for the dominant Muslim religion of the area, mini-skirts and shorts were not worn by tourists. Due to the narrow streets, automobiles were not allowed:—the town was easily explored on foot, bicycle or by donkey. The locals favored the ass!

Another feature of Malindi, that isn't well known, is the numerous Albino people that live there. Many white-haired, red-eyed, topless women strolled the streets, without experiencing strict taboos that would face them in modernized cities. The Albino people, "mixed-in" with the general populace, in this very unique town.

Without making a hotel reservation, we pushed further north to Lamu, only to discover, that outside of a few tourist dress shops, it would require us to book a small boat, with a funny name—dhow—to be taken to the rest of Lamu, that was on an island.

Sue said, "I really don't think we have the time, nor are we prepared to go to the island to see more of Lamu. Maybe some other time, Dear."

"Yes, I guess we better turn around and start back to Kampala. We could stop at either the Tsavo or Amboselli Game Parks and stay in one of their Lodges tonight. What do you all say to that?"

I regretted that decision not to further explore more of the Lamu settlement:—Kenya's oldest inhabited town. It's an original Swahili settlement and is now, a UNESCO World Heritage Site. It's the oldest and best-preserved Swahili settlement, in East Africa. It has several museums, dedicated to the Swahili culture.

The rest of the Lamu town is on Lamu Island, which is part of the Lamu Archipelago. There are interesting tales, of Zhueng He's fleet sinking near Lamu Island. Survivors, settled on the island and married local women. DNA testing performed on some Lamu residents shows they have Chinese ancestors.

Lamu has existed for at least a thousand years. Historical findings were attained from the Arabian traveler, Abu-al-Mahasini, whose writings included, his meeting with a Judge, from Lamu, visiting Mecca in 1441.

The town's history is marked by a Portuguese invasion in 1506 and the Omani domination around 1813—the year of the Battle of Shela.

The Portuguese invasion was prompted by that nation's successful mission to control trade along Kenya's Indian Ocean coast. For a considerable time, Portugal had a monopoly in shipping along the East African coast and imposed export taxes on the pre-existing local channels of distribution. In 1580, Lamunians, along with Turkish men, led a rebellion against the Portuguese. In 1652, Lamunians, assisted by men from Oman, finally rid themselves of Portuguese control. Lamu's years as an Omani protectorate mark the town's Golden Age. Lamu became a centre of poetry, politics, arts and crafts, as well as trade.

Lamu's economy was based on the Slave Trade:—until its abolition in 1907. Other traditional exports were ivory, mangrove, turtle shells and rhinoceros horns. These were shipped, via the Indian Ocean, to the Middle East and India. In addition to the abolition of slavery, construction of the Ugandan Railroad in 1901 significantly hampered Lamu's economy. The UR was started from the competing port of Mombassa.

In recent times, tourism has gradually refueled the local economy of Lamu. China has begun feasibility studies to transform Lamu into the largest port in East Africa, as part of their "String of Pearls" strategy.

In 2011, proposals were being advanced to build a deep-water port that would have much greater capacity in terms of depth of water, number of berths and ability for vessels to arrive and depart at the same time, than Kenya's main port of Mombassa.

"AN UNCROWDED BEACH:"—LAURA AND K.C.,
IN WHITE SAND, ON MOMBASSA BEACH.

"INDIAN OCEAN BREEZES:"—LEO AND K.C., IN KITENGE SHIRTS, BEHIND GERMAN HOTEL, IN MALINDI.

SAFARI 23

We learned:—Nairobi is 5,450 feet above sea level and has a temperate climate, from a high of 76 degrees Fahrenheit to a low of 60 degrees Fahrenheit.

Many of the world's best middle and long distance runner hail from Kenya, because that nation's altitude and climate. It's, "runner-friendly."

Nairobi is located in the highlands of the southern part of Kenya:—an area once frequented by the pastoral Masai tribe.

Nairobi was founded in the late 1890's as a British railroad camp on the Mombassa, Kenya to Kampala, Uganda railroad line.

From 1899 to 1905, Nairobi served as a British provincial capital. In 1905, the city of Nairobi became the capital of the British East Africa Protectorate. From 1920 till 1963, it was capital, in a territory known Kenya Colony.

In 1963, Nairobi became the capital of independent Kenya and annexed neighboring areas, for future growth.

Nairobi manufactures clothing, textiles, building materials, and processes food, beverages, such as coffee and tea, as well as, cigarettes. Nairobi is a transportation hub.

During the 20th Century, Kenya had become a popular safari spot attracting world leaders such as American President Theodore Roosevelt, British Prime Minister Winston Churchill and the Duke of Glouster.

Therefore, Nairobi laid claim to the title of:—"World's Greatest Safari Capital."

So, in 1952, when Elizabeth, then a princess and her new husband, the Duke of Edinburgh, were looking for a perfect vacation spot, they picked, the colony of Kenya. After they visited Nairobi and went on a five-day safari, the couple stayed at the world famous, Treetops Lodge, where many famous Hollywood stars have vacationed.

On the morning of February 6, 1952, King George IV died. Elizabeth went into the Treetops, as a Princess and left as a Queen.

Her Coronation was held more than a year later, on June 1st, 1953.

To celebrate Queen Elizabeth II and Kenya's new place in the royal History, Kenyans inaugurated an auto road race, through the bush. The event was originally called the East African Coronation Rally.

It began in Nairobi and was timed to finish, at the same moment Queen Elizabeth II was crowned, in Westminster Abbey, in London, England.

Hence, the first East African Coronation Rally was a thousand mile race that started on May 27th and ended on June 1st, 1953.

In 1974, this car rally would become an annual event, with its name changed to the East African Safari Rally. It is Kenya's most popular sporting event and Africa's longest car rally:—the only African event on the World Rally Circuit.

This trip, we stayed at Kampala's affiliated Private Club in Nairobi. Sue, Laura and KC spent the days swimming in the pool and trying to get a better suntan.

Since I had been raised in a racehorse family, I decided to attend again the Ngong, Nairobi's only English Thoroughbred racetrack.

While stretching my legs around the area, I met an old Swahili horseman, Joel Nasaburu.

Joel said, "Bwana Cuba (which means big man in Swahili), when you go to the racecourse, do you carry a rabbit's foot, for luck?"

"No, I don't, but I have heard of that African custom practiced by many big game hunters, on Safari, as well as some race-goers."

"Then, let me take you out on a midnight hunt for the special white rabbit, that will bring you many, many treasures. Tonight, we will hunt by the light of a full moon. I have a small fee for such a trip. Very small, Bwana Cuba."

"Okay, only if it's not more than ten shillings (one Canadian dollar). Why does it have to be at midnight by the light of a full moon?"

"Because that is when the magic of the rabbit's foot is at its highest power. Oh, yes Bwana Cuba, it would be best if you wore just a loincloth for the hunt."

"It gets pretty cool here at night doesn't it? Aren't animals and snakes out in the dark?"

"Bwana Cuba would be wise to wear high-ankle socks and boots so the snakes cannot strike. I will protect you from the animals," said Joel.

The weather station predicted a full moon on the night we arrived.

"Okay, Joel—let's do it tonight, at the stroke of midnight," I said.

Relentlessly, Joel had reminded me that I should not be late for our appointment, at the Nairobi Cemetery Park. It had to be, just before midnight. He brought a single-barreled rifle and a panga (machete).

He said, "I have but three slugs that I cut from pig iron lead and I have marked a cross on each one of them. We must sit on the grave of an African Indigenous man, who died at the age of forty-five. No dark clouds must obscure Luna's fair face. Her ghostly radiance, will lighten up the tombstones and a slanting ray will strike the church."

"Okay, okay, it is 11:55, so let's get started," I said.

The fully clothed, Joel retorted, "No, no, we must start exactly at midnight, Bwana Cuba. No sooner or later. You must sit crosswise, over the correct grave, while I journey out to scout for the rabbit."

At exactly midnight, we started our trek, over the dark-and-hilly cemetery compound. We were hunting, one white jackrabbit.

After securing the gun from Joel, I nervously sat down on the face of the grave and "Bam. Click. Bam. Click."

I said, "Oops, I think I just missed that lurking shadow over to my left. I thought it was a spitting cobra getting ready to strike."

"Please be more patient, Bwana Cuba. Do not fire, at just anything. Now, we have only one shot left for the white rabbit," said Joel.

"But Joel, I don't want a poisonous snake striking me or become a midnight snack for a lion or leopard."

"Be patient and trust me, Bwana Cuba. I will be able to hear and smell them, before they can approach you. I know this terrain, like the back of my wrist. Alas, we have only one shot left. If you waste it, we will have to go back to our home lodgings and return another night, but only if all the signs are like tonight—right?" said Joel.

"Okay, Joel. I'll be less trigger happy and trust you more, but please make sure your hearing and smelling apparatus are keen."

An hour went by. Nothing but shadows. Yes, lurking shadows behind tombstones. Strange noises and shrieks filled the air. Strong smells stuffed my nose. I felt the hair on the back of my neck going up, more than once. Still, I did not discharge the gun.

I kept thinking:—patience. Patience wins out.

The hours seemed to drag by. Sunrise came and we were just ready to trek back to our home base, when there was something hopping along, over 50 yards to my right.

I blinked my eyes. My throat got dry. My finger twitched on the trigger. Yes, I saw an air-born, white streak. I aimed two feet to the front of it, and "Bam, click."

The game flipped in the air and landed with a thud, on the ground.

"Yippee," I yelled, as I just shot a big, white jackrabbit. Joel, with his panga in hand, had the hare bagged, ready for cutting.

With great skill, Joel cut off all four feet and handed them to me. He had slit the jackrabbit's throat and said, "I will skin the rabbit and cook him for my family's supper, Bwana Cuba."

"That's fine with me, Joel. Here's 30 shillings for you. It was a long night and you stayed till the job was done. Now, I have my lucky charms."

"Yes, Bwana Cuba. You will win at the Ngong course, tomorrow."

I went back to the hotel, showered, put on clean clothes, swallowed some citrus drink, kissed my wife and kids and headed off to the racecourse, without sleeping a wink.

African Pearls and Poisons

For the first race, I went to the bookie I thought paid off the best returns and, after getting the odds, plunked down fifty shillings on the nose of race favorite, number seven, Starlight.

Starlight ran like a slow dog (slower than a horse) and I wasn't sure if he'd finished the race yet, as the others were back in the barn after being cooled out (walked till their hot blood cooled down).

The next race, I bet Number one, Simba King, with 100 shillings straight (to win.) Simba King ran out of the money. He was also:—an also ran.

"Drat. I'd better put 200 shillings on the favorite in the Kenya Derby, The Sultan. He should handle this field with ease."

The Sultan went to the front of the pack, but ran out of air in the stretch and came in a gasping second to last.

I muttered, "So much for superstition. Joel's a nice guy but this rabbit's foot thing is hocus-pocus. Yes, just smoke-and-mirrors."

With that, I tossed the four rabbit's feet into the garbage barrel and left the racecourse, for our hotel.

Sue asked me, "How did you do at the racetrack?"

I said, "My luck was consistent. It was all bad."

"So, this lucky rabbit's foot thing didn't work," she chided.

"No, it didn't. I tossed them away."

The next morning we packed the car up and went to a restaurant for breakfast. While dining, we overheard the familiar voice of an Englishman, in conversation at the table next to ours.

"Egad. Did I ever get lucky at Ngong yesterday! I wasn't doing any good until the fourth race, when I picked up four rabbit's feet out of the garbage, as I was going to the exit. I swung right around and put a thousand shillings on horse number four and he came in, with boxcar (more than ten) numbers. Breakfast is on me this morning."

My stomach went topsy-turvy. I nearly lost my breakfast. I turned around, to see who was doing the talking. It was, "The Pale Rat," who squealed to "a Poisonous Viper."

SAFARI 24

Heading toward the Tsavo East, one of the largest game reserves in the world, we left Nairobi, and drove in the shadow of Africa's second highest mountain, Mount Kenya. During the journey, I just couldn't get, 'The Pale Rat,' out of my mind.

After a couple hours, I stopped the car, in a highway "pull-off," for lunch. While eating, I took out my notebook and read what I'd previously written down in my main interview notebook about this traitor to mankind, 'The Pale Rat,' Bob Ames.

At the request of Tom Williams, Editor of, the Ugandan Argus (The Voice of Africa) newspaper, and as an Investigative Reporter, I had conducted a 1971 interview with Colonel Bob Ames, Manager of Uganda Television.

The East Indian pipeline noted:—"Ames had been the chief informer (rat) on the Acholi and Langi (Obote's light-skinned sympathizers) tribesmen who were put in prison cells, subsequently dynamited. Any survivors of that blast were beaten to death by old and rusted lorry axels in Kampala's Makindye Prison.

From that moment on, Ames was widely known as 'the Pale Rat.'

He was Amin's trusty sidekick and informed on people to the notorious killing group, Ames had dubbed, "The State Research Bureau." They were said to be a poisonous group of men who showed no mercy. Ames liked to embarrass the Brits.

I re-read my notes:

December 15, 1971—

The Pale Rat (Colonel Bob Ames), Englishman, mid-forties, slight build, blond, balding, under six feet, 150 lbs.; unsmiling, intense manner.

L.J.—"Could you tell me about your army background and how you became a Colonel?"

P.R.—"When I was 21, I joined the British Indian Army and rose to the rank of lieutenant. I dubbed myself, 'Colonel Bob,' to show my true worth."

L.J.—"Why did you join the British Indian Army?"

P.R.—"I was young and wanted to see the world, I guess. I enjoyed being with other nationalities and taking part in their fights."

L.J.—"How did you come to settle in Uganda?"

P.R.—"I came to Uganda in 1949 and was a player in Ugandan politics. My English wife and I had divorced. I married Mary, an aristocratic member of the then governing Bugandan tribe. I succeeded in planning the defeat of the other tribes, who were rising in rebellion against the Bugandans, who were backed by England. For my service, the British appointed me Colonial Officer with the Ministry of Works."

L.J.—"Then what?"

P.R.—"As a Colonial Officer, I built the Uganda Aviation Services Limited. It was the first airline to employ Indigenous African Ugandans. When Milton Obote's Acholi tribe defeated our Bugandan tribe and took over the running of the government from the British in 1961, the U.A.S. was nationalized. I was fortunate to be valued and hired as Special Advisor to President Obote. In fact, we were so close that when now President Amin took over on January 1st, 1971, he called me a 'rotten apple,' and I was jailed in Makindye Prison from the first of January, 1971 till April 15, 1971."

L.J.—"How were you yourself treated while in Makindye Prison?"

P.R.—"Roughly. I was knocked about—floored by the guards. In fact, one of the guards who helped pick me up after a beating was himself kicked to death."

L.J.—"But, you survived while many Acholi, loyal to Obote, lost their lives in Makindye. How come?"

P.R.—"President Amin realized that I was not a follower of the evil Milton Obote or his conniving, Acholi tribe. Amin noted that I possessed many qualities that would help him lead Uganda in its war against Obote and his tribe for control. Amin understood he could trust me to give him honest assessments of people and situations, that would help him deal with other countries, especially Britain."

After reading through my notes, I drove on towards our destination. I couldn't help reflecting on those notes I made then, as I do now.

'The Pale Rat' was the main creator of the Amin persona, for the Western Alliance, portraying him as a buffoon—a bumbling clown of a man—rather than the sly, slimy, cowardly, criminal butcher he really was.

It was "The Pale Rat," who primed Amin to come up with the tirade of irksome insults towards England, all British-born and trained people, except himself, of course.

In the movie, "The Last King of Scotland," there was a fictitious "Pale Rat" shown with Kay Amin.

We met the real Kay Amin, during to her and Amin's visit to the Uganda College of Commerce, on September 15, 1972. Kay was an ever-smiling and gracious lady.

In real life, Kay had an affair, and a resulting pregnancy, with a medical doctor. The doctor tried to perform an abortion on Kay, of the result from their union.

Kay died during the operation and the doctor cut her body into pieces in order to make it easier for him to depose of his wrong doings.

He then had his own wife and their five children take poison, as he also did, and they all died. Poison kills!

Amin was furious when he was informed of what the doctor had done as well as having found Kay cut up in pieces. Amin had Kay's body parts shown back together into a gruesome sight. Then, he had his other wives and his children view the extremely disturbing sight of Kay's mutilated body as he tried to make a point to those assembled.

Amin said, "See the judgment of Allah on a bad, bad Christian woman."

SAFARI 25

Sue cut into my reflections and said, "You seem to be caught up in going over your notes and daydreaming, Leo. Could you please get your mind away from your work, or whatever else you were thinking about, and back on our family vacation."

I said, "Okay. Now how large did you say this Tsavo Game Park is?"

"It says, in this guide book, it's ten million square miles," said Sue.

"Wow! That would make it as big as the entire island of Jamaica where our friends, Peter and Monika Trunk live."

"Yes and it has all the African animals anyone would want to see."

It wasn't long before we had arrived at the circular Tsavo East Game Lodge with its base is made out of volcanic stone surrounded by a veranda enclosed with lush, flowers, foliage and hanging bird cages.

World famous Mount Kilimanjaro, the highest mountain in Africa, provided the backdrop. It is Africa's highest mountain and Mount Kenya the second tallest.

The Tsavo Game Park was established when the British made a concentrated effort to colonize the interior of Kenya in the late 19th Century.

In 1898, they built a railway through Tsavo. Legend had it:—that "man-eating lions," terrorized and fed on members of the construction crew.

The 1986 book, "The Man-Eaters of Tsavo," by Colonel J. M. Patterson formed the basis for the 1996 movie, "The Ghost and the Darkness," starring Michael Douglas. It told about this experience, as was a follow-up 2003 book, "The Lions of Tsavo: Exploring the Legacy of Africa's Notorious Man-Eaters," by Bruce Patterson.

Modern research indicates:—the Waata tribe, indigenous to the area, was hostile to the railway and more-than-likely committed the kidnapping and killing of some of the railway employees.

We experienced the local culture of a traditional Masai Village. The villagers live simply, making their homes in round boma huts constructed from mud and sticks.

Sue got a great picture of a Masai woman in all her splendor. One Masai man stood tall (near 7 feet), with an ever-ready spear, at his side.

I thought:—That guy would make a great centre in a game of basketball.

We were enjoying a leisure day at the Tsavo East Lodge, with the red and gold flowers. Exquisite humming-birds were everywhere. Laura and KC were enjoying feeding, these birds and the gecko lizards, the English scones from our dinner plates.

We had been on safari in the Park and had enjoyed seeing the lions, elephants, black rhinoceros and the bands of zebras, wildebeests, and all types of antelopes. We had also observed a band of baboon and different species of monkeys. Wild animals, in vast numbers, were everywhere. We continuously saw a stunning array of wildlife from antelopes and gnus to warthogs and zebras.

Our favorite game animal was the giraffe and we saw two species of this marvelous, long-necked stroller, as they devoured foliage, off the top of the forest trees.

From a distance, we had seen the hippopotami band, as they lolled and grunted, half-submerged, among the giant lily pads in the river.

I had thought: It would be neat to have been up closer to them, so we could get better pictures, but our jeep driver, on seeing them, quickly pushed on muttering, "They are unpredictable and can charge faster than a rhino."

I said, "It doesn't make sense to me. The hippo is a water animal, mostly. At least, that's where we've chiefly seen them. They surely don't look built for speed. I think I could outrun a hippo. In high school track, I ran a 5:06 mile and a 1:52 half-mile. I don't think a hippo can run that far, at that speed."

Our driver said, "It would be wise for you to not test your theory, Bwana Cuba."

The day went on and we returned to the Lodge. As darkness started to fall, KC accompanied me down to a bridge overlooking a placid stream.

As we watched the sun slip slowly down under the horizon, we simultaneously spied a mother hippopotamus and her baby calf. They were sauntering out of the stream and up the bank towards where we were standing.

KC was thrilled to see these two "river-horses," coming closer. The baby hippo was especially cute, wobbling back and fro, with its little, fat legs.

Something in my gut, told me it was time to hurriedly depart back up the bank to the Lodge. The Lodge was about 300 yards away.

It was then, mother hippo, throwing her head from side to side, started her charge.

She made a deep, laughing roar that sent shivers up my spine and got me going.

I grabbed up KC, spun around, hurdled the Lodge's barrier wall and made a dash for the sliding glass door on the veranda.

We arrived at the door and we were inside it and up the stairway just before mother hippo had flattened the barrier, and came to a sudden, screeching stop, as she slammed into the side of the Lodge's veranda.

Showing some minor cuts to her tough skin, the irate mother stomped her massive feet and bellowed like a bull, at a high pitch. Her calf was hovered at her side.

Circling the veranda, Mother Hippo made some menacing movements and sounds towards the rest of the building. She, and baby, circled the entire building and returned.

Then, after dusting herself off by shaking her massive body, she quickly turned their direction around, and with both their tails held high, ran off into the night.

The Lodge Manager was the first person to come down the stairway. He had equipped himself with what looked like an elephant rifle.

He went outside and fired his gun off in the air.

He came back into the Lodge, and said, "Bwana Cuba should not test his running skill against a hippo. Hippos have killed more people in Kenya than any other wild animal. I trust you will reimburse me for any damage you have caused."

I nodded and said, "Yes, I'll pay for the cost of my ignorance."

He said, "Many times, humans make a fatal mistake because they think hippos are cute and clumsy and can't catch them."

I said, "Yes. Fuzzy thinking could lead to being one's last thoughts."

Next morning, we packed up and hurriedly headed back to our College home.

CHAPTER FIVE
COOL MOUNTAINS OF THE MOON

SAFARI 26

For this Christmas, I thought of the Swahili saying:—"May your troubles be less, your blessings more and nothing but happiness, come through your door."

Two weeks before our first Christmas in Uganda, we received a letter from Arusha, Tanzania (a town at the foot of Mt. Kilimanjaro). It was from Bob Zach, a 33 year-old, fellow Canadian from Calgary who was serving CIDA in Arusha, with his pregnant wife, Flo, 32, their daughter, Penny, three and Bob's mother, Jean 65 years old.

They were traveling first to Kampala Uganda for a Christmas break en route to the Mountains of the Moon (the Rheuwenzoris range) along the border of southwest Uganda and then to Zaire (now named The Democratic Republic of the Congo).

Bob wanted to know if we, as a family, would like to set up a Christmas dinner for them in or around Kampala and join them on their three-week travel tour.

We quickly wired back our affirmative reply.

Bob was a Science teacher at a centralized mid-grade school for boys, in Arusha. He taught Grade Seven Science and was interested in hunting all the wild game in Africa.

He had already shot:—an Impala and a Wildebeest—in Tanzania. He had not brought his gunfire along, on this Safari.

While Bob was relating to us his hunting expeditions, I thought back to having read about how American President Theodore Roosevelt had shot a trophy of every animal in Africa on his safaris, while preaching about wildlife preservation in the United States. Roosevelt was responsible for many large game parks in America.

We booked three rooms at the swank Lake Victoria Hotel from Christmas Eve till Boxing Day (the day after Christmas) and arranged for Christmas Day dinner in the hotel dining room. This lovely hotel was:—a mixture of white stucco and red tile, with old cobblestone walkways, surrounded by African palm trees and giant land tortoises.

It was like an oasis in the jungle, with massive growth all around it. It had an Olympic sized pool, with cabanas and shaded-lawn chairs and sunk on marbled tiles, within a red brick with iron rod fence.

The hotel staff kept a three-to-one ratio of assistants to guests, causing a slight commotion, with a trio trying to be the one to help you, in any way possible.

The Zach's arrived at the Uganda College of Commerce compound two days before Christmas and after spending the first night with us at our place, in make-shift living arrangements, followed us in their Peugeot to Entebbe and the Lake Victoria Hotel. The evening before leaving, we discussed with Bob and Flo the three-room arrangement we had made with the Hotel. They preferred to cancel one room as well as stay just one night (Christmas Eve) at the Hotel, so we could start our travels early, on Christmas Day. They wanted to get on the road, as soon as possible.

We had no idea what the buffet menu was at the Lake Victoria Hotel and wondered if they had turkeys in Uganda as we hadn't seen or heard of any.

The only time we had heard the word "turkey," used, was three weeks before, when an expatriate Canadian had rushed into our home and loudly boldly said, "Let's talk turkey. Do you want some turkey?"

We sat stunned, and, looking bewildered, replied, "Do you mean for Christmas dinner?" He laughed and said, "No. Do you want discounted Uganda Shillings at 12 to one for your Canadian dollar?"

I replied, "Isn't that black marketing?"

He spouted, "Wow! You catch on fast. Well then, how much do you want? My contact can handle any amount you name on a daily, weekly or monthly basis. I'm leaving Uganda soon and I'll put you in touch with this contact right away. What's your pleasure?"

I looked him straight in the eye and said, "We're here to help the Ugandan people and not to benefit by using black market money. We aren't interested in your offer. Please leave the premises."

He smiled and uttered, "You're making a big mistake. You'll regret your decision because the Uganda Shilling is a way overvalued at the banks. You're the first expatriate I've offered my turkey to that has refused it."

He went on, "I only make only 10 shillings per dollar for putting you in touch with the mother lode, an Ismaili East Indian duka owner."

"That's very interesting but we decline. We'll abide by the bank's exchange," I said and closed the door behind him.

At the Lake Victoria Hotel's Christmas buffet, there was no turkey. On a carving table:—was one gigantic pink wild boar, with an apple in his mouth, and a smiling East Indian Chef sharpening his large knife for the cutting.

All around the room were staple and mysterious vegetables and scrumptious salads, as well as a massive selection of weight-gaining desserts, including five kinds of pies and five kinds of cakes. It was a meal fit for royalty and was kicked off with a delicious soup and biscuits.

In the five months since arriving in Kampala, we had eaten very little meat because of the unhealthy way it hung with flies all over it, in the market place.

On enquiry as to the butchering of animals, we were told; it was very unsanitary in all of East Africa and to refrain from eating any butchered meat.

Therefore, we had eaten mostly fish, fresh market vegetables, salads and fruits and every one of us in the family, had lost at least ten pounds of weight.

During our Christmas Eve dining at the Lake Vic Hotel (as it was known), we all engaged in eating some pork that night, only to terribly regret it, months later.

Christmas Day came and we all exchanged simple presents we could use on our trip.

After an early breakfast, we all had a short swim, then loaded up the two cars: our, Volkswagen Fastback and their, Peugeot.

SAFARI 27

Once we left the Kampala-Entebbe paved road we drove along the red murrain (dust) road towards, "the Switzerland of Africa:"—the southwestern corner of Uganda.

The scenery was lush, with lots of different shades of green and red. There were many foothills, backed by the Mountains in the Moon in the background, and valleys where the coffee, tea and other crops grew up to the terraced highlands.

The most significant aspect of Southwestern Uganda is the coolness in the air and one being able to breathe much easier. The daytime temperature dropped twenty degrees from the ordinary 75 degrees above Fahrenheit.

Yes, it invigorated us, as it was what we were used to on a May Day in Calgary, Alberta. For the first time, in a long time, the engrossing temperature was the topic of conversation, on our first day of travel.

Along the trail-like road, we had to stop many times for herded longhorn, Acholi cattle. They looked very much like Texas longhorns.

A collie dog helped the shoeless tribal herdsman, keep the cattle on the course towards the slaughterhouse, in the biggest town around, Kabale.

At Kabale, the locals will engage you in conversation about zero grazing, beekeeping, mushroom growing, flower farming and Ugandan handicrafts and art.

Tin roofed shantytown, Kabale had not, "an acceptable to our women," Hotel, Motel or Inn, to stay at. Darkness fell quickly around five o'clock, and it would be dangerous for us to drive too much further.

We were informed by Game Warden, Isaac Newton to seek overnight accommodation, at an old house just outside of town.

An expatriate English couple, Mr. and Mrs. John Hunt owned the house and offered overnight accommodation, for the reasonable rate of 49 shillings (seven dollars) a night. The Lake Victoria Hotel had been ten times that amount. Hence, we were happy to settle down at the Hunt's for a night.

Everyone seemed to enjoy having a break from the day's travel. We enjoyed an English style supper of a milky and doughy mix of little pieces of meat with vegetables, like steak and kidney pie.

A hot berry pie, with homemade ice cream, especially pleased Laura, KC and Penny. The adults enjoyed a flavorful blend of tea.

Mr. Hunt smoked a pipe and related stories of the past achievements of the British Empire and, "How we go back to London to see how things are being run, every five years or so. We are glad that we live here in this temperate climate."

He was interested in our assignments and how we could help the indigenous Africans.

Mr. Hunt interrupted my thoughts and said, "Most of the indigenous Africans haven't seen most of Uganda's wildlife, or do they really care about their demise in their country. The only benefit they see:—is how it attracts tourist dollars to them."

I inquired, "Why don't they care about the wildlife outside of the tourist dollars they bring in? Please explain."

"Well, they are trying to farm and some animals like the elephants and rhinos trample their crops. The birds try to pick their crops clean before harvest. It's also dangerous with lions, snakes and the likes being around."

After Bob excused himself, for an early rise tomorrow, Mr. Hunt shared with me some of his thoughts about the African indigenous shopkeeper.

He said, "The Ugandan-born, African shopkeeper has to overcome the expectations of the rural indigenous, who want everything now and on credit. It places him, as the shopkeeper, in a very difficult position."

I asked, "How do you think the indigenous shopkeeper should be trained?"

Mr. Hunt answered, "Firstly, he needs to identify himself with the struggle for independence from his former bosses, be they East Indian, British or otherwise. His patriotic ideal should be, to gain the respect for African society internationally."

I asked, "In your opinion, what kind of education or training should this indigenous shopkeeper have?"

"He should have an above average education, but not sufficient to secure an influential, salaried position, with prestige. As a result, he turns to business to gain independence and to be master of his own achievements."

I queried, "What about the practice of employing relatives?"

"Yes, there is an extended family here in Uganda. It's part of East African Socialism. The practice of partnerships, between members of different families, is rare, in East Africa. The concept of a family business to an Indigenous, in the European or East Indian model, is alien to the Indigenous African."

Why are the majority of the shopkeepers in Uganda, East Indian?"

"Serving in a duka (store), to an East Indian child, is as natural as herding goats, for an East African child. Don't forget, that wealth, in an East African Society, is distributed to each son, as he comes to manhood. He is not taught, to learn to earn, at an early age."

"Thank you, Mr. Hunt, for your viewpoints. They enlighten me, on the road we must travel, to make indigenous Ugandans successful shopkeepers."

I went to our room. Sue and the kids were already asleep.

I looked out the window at the sunset. It was as brilliant as a Ugandan indigenous' smile, that is scribbled with the stunning liquidity of iridescent gold, topaz and ruby, that just melts into nightfall.

To me, the loveliest part of Uganda is the District of Kigezi, where the Hunt's home lies.

Nearby, there are rushing rivers in deep valleys, steep hills, marked to their very tops, with squares of civilization:—blue-green patches of peas and beans, the darker green of bananas and dotted with little groups of huts, granaries and cattle pens.

After filling up the cars with petrol (gas), we left the next morning on the steep road over bamboo-clad ridges, for the Mountains of the Moon Inn, at the bottom of Margherita Mountain, of the snow-capped Mountains of the Moon.

Here, we would stay the night and later meet are part-Hutu and part-Pygmy guide, from Kigali, Rwanda, to go up the mountain and meet with the Twa Pygmy Tribe in the Ituri Rainforest, in Zaire, Central Africa.

The temperature was a brisk fifty degrees Fahrenheit, as we drove along the bumpy, red murrain road, watching the wildlife, in the form of Uganda Kob (Impalas) and wild boars scampering, along the trail.

Our family struck up a singsong, along the way and enjoyed the crispness of the Canadian-like climate. The sky was a purplish-blue, with some slight traces of white clouds. The heavens opened up with rain for five minutes, then stopped and in the next five minutes, all traces of water had disappeared:—sucked up into the bright red soil.

The Mountains of the Moon Inn was a beautiful kept, converted three-story Victorian style house run by two delightful middle-aged, Scottish people, James and Beatrice McDuke. On their land, a giant lilac tree dwarfed our yellow Volkswagen.

The McDukes knew the Hunts and asked about their health. After we exchanged pleasantries and got our bags to our rooms, we enjoyed Mrs. McDuke's scrumptious meal of Potato and Beet Stew, with tea to drink and cup cakes for dessert.

The McDukes, formerly from Edinburgh, had operated the Mountain of the Moons Inn, for the past ten years.

"Yes, Bea does all the cooking for our guests, the servant do all the landscaping and I help you plan out your trip up the mountain," said James, with a smile on his red face. "I best warn you right now, that you best listen to my advice, or pay the price."

I asked, "What do you mean by that, Mr. McDuke? Is their some danger we should know about?"

James said, "Well then, now that I've got you attention, Mr. Jacques and Mr. Zach, come over and sit in the chairs around me and I'll tell you how to avoid trouble, with a capital T."

He said, "The name, Pygmy comes from the Greek word, 'Pugmaios'—meaning a cubit tall. Homer described, in his writings, the Pugmaios tribe's fight with the Cranes."

James picked up a book by Homer:—The Iliad 3, 3 ff (trans. Lattimore) (Greek epic C8th B.C.) and read:—"The clamour of cranes goes high to the heavens, when the cranes escape the winter time and the rains unceasing and clamorously wing their way to streaming Okeanos (Oceanus), bringing the Pygmaioi (Pygmy) men bloodshed and destruction:—at daybreak they bring on the baleful battle against them."

He added, "It is believed the Pugmaios (Pygmies) to be one of the oldest, if not the oldest, race in the world.

As a race, the Pugmaios (Pygmies) were depicted on Egyptian pottery 4,000 years ago. Pepi II Neferkare, the last king of the 6th dynasty (2325BC-2150BC) had pygmies."

Bob and I, alertly listened, as he revealed to us this history and the unwritten rules, when visiting the Twa Pygmies, of the Ituri Rainforest.

James stated, "The Twa Pygmies have all but been driven out of Burundi and Rwanda, where they once very were prevalent. They live, a semi-nomadic existence, in Uganda's western region and mainly in the Ituri Rainforest Area of Zaire."

He added, "The reason you will be guided by a part-Hutu, part-Twa Pygmy guide on your safari is part of an agreement by you to hire a part-Tutsi, part-Pygmy guide to the Queen Elizabeth Park on your next safari. Furthermore, you must pay both guides their fee, as well as pay the Twa Pygmies, for any pictures you take."

I asked, "Why do we pay for pictures taken?"

James said, "The Twa Pygmies contend, that your taking pictures of them has taken part of their soul, just like an X-ray machine may radiate off cancerous rays. Hence, you must pay an agreed on price before you take any pictures."

Bob asked, "What do we do about our young ones? Will they be safe when we visit the pygmies?"

James said, "That's a good question, Bob. I would advise you to keep the young ones, in your vehicles, with the doors locked and the windows rolled up. I know that may sound a bit inhumane, but you must be aware that these pygmies are a bit savage and have been known to kidnap children."

I asked, "Is there anything else we should know?"

217

James said, "Yes, there is. Make sure, you devise danger signs to communicate among you. If you start to feel unsafe, be sure to signal the others and try to stick together. I suggest you have a whistle around your necks to blow. Don't go far from your guide or the group. These Twa Pygmies are known, as great hunters, possessing great skill with poison arrows."

I asked, "How many times have you ventured up to see the tribe?"

"Oh, I've been up there at least twenty times and have always gone with a guide. I have never had any trouble, but others have, who don't heed me and my knowledge of these unique peoples."

After thanking our hosts, we met with our Guide, Tomas Homru and started our cars, on the safari up Mount Margherita, of the Mountains of the Moon, on roads, that were nothing more than, bumpy, narrow survival trails.

Our Safari guide, Tomas Homru, was a 22 year old, born to a Twa Pygmy mother and a Hutu tribe father. Tomas had been reared in a small settlement in Kigali, Rwanda. Tomas smelled like raw Canadian bacon. He was a little over five feet tall, with a scar in the wrinkles near his left eye. It seemed to cause Tomas to continuously squint.

I estimated Tomas's height, to be 5 foot, 2 inches and weight to be in:—the 130 to 140 lb. range.

His wiry hair was cut close to his head and he was dressed in a western style, grayish shirt and denim jeans. His manner was stern and abrupt, then apologetic, when he sensed, to have made a mistake.

Tomas said, "By retreating into Zaire's forests, the Twa Pygmies, have managed to retain their physical peculiarities of ugliness and their nomadic way of life."

In the shadows, smeared visions of Twa Pygmies, could be glimpsed or imagined—shy, silent, watchful. We're in their world, dismantled and repackaged, by our Guide.

At 8,000 feet, our cars steamed up and sore assed, from all the bumps, we stopped by the steep ledge, to let a little Twa girl, carrying a heavy load on her head, pass us. Sue snapped a picture of the little Twa girl.

Tomas said, "Please Memsahib (European married woman) Sue, do not take pictures of the Twa without me first negotiating the price of such a picture. They believe, when you take their picture you take part of their soul and they want to be paid for all the pictures you take."

He added, "She is just a girl. Females do not negotiate the price. Only men can do that. Women are only good for two things:—work and sex!"

Tomas's opinion drew a stony look from Sue.

He added, "Oh, I apologize Memsab Jacques, I didn't mean to include Memsab such as yourself when I make statement."

Sue answered, "Where did you get that attitude towards women, Tomas? Do you realize that you are putting down all women, when you make such a statement?"

Tomas was a silent as a stone. He stared out the window and fiddled with his hands. His face was twisted and he looked dumbfounded. His glance towards me demanded:—Why don't you control your woman?

I said nothing. He was on his own.

The silence in the car was deafening. I could hear the pounding in my eardrums grow louder and louder like the drum beats hunters use to drive a scared animal to a trap or ambush.

Sweat covered my brow so I rolled down the driver's window.

The kids in the back seats of the car had nodded off.

My two companions up front, Sue and Tomas were acting like the other one wasn't there.

Suddenly, the stony silence changed.

SAFARI 28

"Herr Help! Herr Help," cried a sobbing, twenty-something woman, clad only in a bra and panties, as she staggered from one side of the road to the other.

Right behind her, was another young damsel, in similar distress and attire.

A bleeding, thirty year-old male, in jockey shorts and trying to regain his feet, was followed by another, scantily clad beaten fellow, just rounding the bend.

I hammered down the brake and swung open the door, while the car was digging in and settling down into the thick, red rock-soil.

Tomas was also out of the car. He was on the path, cowering beside the door, on the other side of our vehicle.

I shouted out, "Who are you? What has happened to you?"

The first woman came towards me and fell into my arms. Sue took the female, in the cradle of her arms, while pulling the sobbing woman's head, to her breast.

By the time I reached second woman, Bob's car had arrived on the scene. Between sobs, screams and yelps, we got a terrifying picture of what had happened.

There was a language barrier. These people were Germans and talking in their native tongue. None of us knew their language, but, from what we could decipher:—the Pygmies had attacked them, for some unknown reason.

"Herr Kopf der Mauser! Herr Kopf der Mauser!" I think the first man said, "Mister get a rifle," or something like that. His eyes were lit up like a volcano.

After a half-hour of trying to attain some semblance of clarity and sanity into the situation, as well as treating the men's wounds and providing blankets to our new acquaintances, we deciphered their story.

They were East Germans from East Berlin.

Three days before, these two East German couples, had met up with the Twa Pygmies. The men were professional photographers and possessed expensive photographic equipment.

Previous to meeting up with the Pygmies, the group of four had also stopped at the Mountains of the Moon Inn and met with James and Beatrice McDuke.

The men had argued with James McDuke, over having to pay the Twa Pygmies for pictures taken.

The couples had left in a huff, and from what we could gather from their account, had met up with the Pygmies and had started taking pictures immediately.

The Pygmies had demanded to be paid for these pictures and when they were denied, a scuffle broke out between the Twa Pygmies and the East Germans.

During the ensuing fight, the East German men were overwhelmed and beaten unconscious, stripped of their cameras, car and accessories, as well as their clothes.

The two women had also lost most of their clothes, but had been spared a bruising beating by the Pygmies and had been allowed to drag their semi-conscious male companions onto the trail and descend the mountain, past an empty Semliki camp, to where they had met us.

For our trip back down Mount Margherita, we decided to change seating arrangements in the two cars and return to the Mountains of the Moon Inn.

Bob took Tomas and our son, KC with his group, which included the rest of the Zach troop. Our daughter, Laura helped Sue look after the two German ladies, in the back seat of our car, while the two battered German men, sat up front with me.

We arrived at the Mountains of the Moon Inn just before dark and the McDukes' took over the rescue operation, providing shelter, food and comfort to all.

James said, "I'll contact the Kigezi District Game Warden, Isaac Newton immediately and arrangements will be made to have these four victims picked up by an ambulance car and taken to the Kabale medical clinic."

James and his wife, Bea efficiently handled the situation and the East Germans were put in an ambulance, to go to the medical clinic in Kabale.

Our group took up another days lodging at the Inn. We all starting mulling over the question:—what would be our next safari?

Next morning, Ben Gantu, a part—(Wa)Tutsi, part-Twa Pygmy Guide from Kigali, Rwanda, arrived, to take over our expedition.

Ben was five inches taller than Tomas, and more than ten pounds heavier.

Ben continually showed his pearly teeth. He spoke softly and bent his head to listen. He seemed genuinely interested in what you were saying to him.

Ben said, "Tomas told me that he was too ill to continue and has asked to be paid out for his time with you."

We settled accounts with Tomas and wished him well.

We had some decisions to make before we totally committed to signing a guide contact with Ben to visit the Twa Pygmies of the Ituri Rainforest in Zaire.

SAFARI 29

The Mountains of the Moon Inn is surrounded by big, Lilac-like bushes the height the size of two tall giraffes. It was a safe haven for everyone.

Now, a decision had to be made. Were we going with Ben to visit to the Twa Pygmies, or stay put, then push on to journey to the Queen Elizabeth Game Park?

Were we asking for trouble if we visited the Pygmies? Maybe the women are right:—the Pygmies may be too dangerous for anyone, let alone a family, to visit.

Our Mountains of the Moon Inn host, James McDuke said, "I think Warden Newton will help you, if he has the time to set it all up. There are a lot of poachers killing off animals in his park, so he may be too occupied with them, to help right away. You're welcome to stay with us for as long as you like. We enjoy your company."

Bob answered, "Our schedule has been thrown off and we'll be lucky to see Queen Elizabeth or Murchison Falls Game Parks if we take too much time trying to see these Twa Pygmies. To me, it seems like we should, but then again, the women aren't much for it, after seeing what happened to the Germans. I sure wish I had my gun."

I asked James, "Have you heard anything more about those poor, German people, who got beat up by the Pygmies?"

"Nothing substantial, except I learned they came to us from Kigali, Rwanda and not what they previously told us:—Kabale, Uganda," said James. "Oh yes, both of the men have broken bones, to go along with a lot of lacerations and bruises. They will probably be in recovery mode for some time. One thing for sure:—They won't be coming back this way anytime soon."

"Do you think the Warden will do anything to the Pygmies and get the Germans stolen goods back?" asked Bob.

"He probably will do that before he does anything to set up a meeting for you with the Pygmy camp."

I asked, "Is the one the Germans visited the only Twa Pygmy camp around here?"

"Afraid so," James uttered. "You're welcome to stay with us for as long as you desire."

I said, "We best have another adult meeting and decide what we're going to do."

I mulled over in my mind:—Maybe, we should use the wireless to get in touch with Warden Newton ourselves.

After supper, Bob and I got the wireless and called Warden Newton, and to our surprise, he answered, "I'm just a little over ten miles away from the Inn and I'll drop in to see you when I get there in a half-hour."

The adults had a quick meeting. The adult women decided to have Sue act as their spokesperson and ask, Warden Newton:—What do you think of our plan of visiting the Twa Pygmies and do you feel it would be safe?

True to his word, Warden Isaac Newton arrived. He had a stern look on his face.

As spokesperson for the women, Sue asked, "Could you accompany us to see them Warden Newton, and if not, could you make the arrangements that we could visit them safely? We'd like your professional opinion, Sir."

Warden Newton said, "I cannot personally go with you. I have already taken a trip up to the Twa Pygmies and they have returned the car and all the equipment and clothes they took from the Germans without anything being damaged beyond repair."

He continued, "Their story is that the black-bearded German kicked an old Pygmy Ma-Ma in the belly and that the tribe defended her and took this man down. The blond haired German, punched and kicked the Chief and therefore he too had to suffer the consequences of his actions."

He went on, "The Pygmies say they are a peaceful tribe. They explained to me, if outsiders like you want to take pictures of them, the cost is fifty Uganda Schillings for each camera. If there are two or more cameras, they are willing to dicker over that price. They believe you take part of their soul when you take a picture of them?"

"Do you believe them, Warden? Do you think they are sincere?" I asked.

He said, "They have always been honest with me. I believe that it's only human nature for these Pygmies to defend their own people. The Twa are proud warriors! They've always been completely up front with me."

Bob said, "I wish you could you accompany us on a trip up to see them. Since you say you will not, then I would like to rent a gun from you."

Warden Newton answered, "I think you'd be safe if you choose to visit them, play by their rules and heed their warnings. I cannot go with you. Your Guide, Ben, is part-Twa and is well respected by this Pygmy tribe. He will act as your intermediary in dealings with them."

He went on, "I advise you to go. They are most interested to meet with you and show you their wares. You do know that they are allowed to hunt any animal in Uganda. They have a lot of unique trinkets to sell you."

"What about renting me a gun" asked Bob?

The Warden answered, "I could rent you a gun, but with no bullets. President Amin has ordered that all bullets are the property of the Uganda Army and we don't even have any to protect us in our work. So, I say your gun idea would be only for show and not a good idea as they would see it as a threat."

I asked, "Would you take your wife and family to see them, Warden?'

"Yes, I would. In my opinion all of you will be safe. The tribe has assured me that you will be welcome. They feel badly as to what occurred with the German couples and want to make friends with anyone who wants to visit and respect them."

I shook Warden Newton's hand, and called for a group meeting.

After much discussion on whether to go or no, the vote was unanimous:—We go! If there should be any sign of problems, we would leave immediately. The women were adamant about this!

At last, we decided to sign on with our new Guide, Ben:—firstly, we'd go with him to Semliki, Uganda and visit with the mountain gorillas, monkeys, and baboons we had heard so much about, and then, we'd visit the Pygmies.

We will take both cars. Our Volkswagen will accommodate all the kids and they will not be allowed to be outside the locked car.

Our 12 year-old daughter, Laura will also stay in our car and baby-sit all the youngsters.

Sue will take pictures with our camera. The Zach's will have two cameras. After a discussion, we agreed that we would split the cost. At fifty schillings a camera, the total cost will be one hundred-and-fifty shillings split down the middle by the two families:—seventy-five shilling apiece (about US$11.)

We all made it an early night at the Mountains of the Moon Inn. At 6 a.m. the next morning, we were on our way ten miles up the Mount Margherita on the bumpy and rocky trail to visit with the Twa Pygmies of Zaire's Ituri Rain forest.

I said, "Sue, I'm exhilarated! This is our chance of a lifetime!"

She said, "Yes dear, but you leave as soon as I signal we leave. Right?"

"Okay."

After less than an hour of chugging up the narrow, winding snail's pace road, Ben advised us, "Rest the car at the side of the path for a little while. There is a hot water pool named, Spider Spa in the forest clearing which you may wish to see."

Sue and I were the only ones interested in going with Ben into the dense rain forest. The temperature was well over 80 degrees Fahrenheit.

Sue said, "I'll come to take pictures of you two, if this spa isn't too far off the road. I'm not promising anything."

I gave Sue a brass whistle to put around her neck so that she could have something to blow in case we got separated and I needed to find her.

"It's just a little ways in," said Ben. "I know exactly where it is."

The forest that had been dark suddenly became lit by streaks of daylight. It was as if heaven had opened up and spotlighted where we were through the dense trees. This jungle wasn't a jungle anymore, but an Eden that took your breath away.

As we kept trudging along, I thought: Joseph Conrad was wrong when he referred to this rain forest as, "The Heart of Darkness."

My overwhelming impression is not of darkness, nor of oppressive gloom, but of life in its most exciting and vibrant form.

I said, "The leaves covering the rain forest's topsoil, turn the water flowing from a stream alongside our path into the color of strong coffee."

Ben said, "These streams can be fed by tropical rain blasts. Lucky for us, we are at the start of the dry season and not subject to having this path washed out by overflowing water."

At Spider spa, I bent down and took some water in my hand and splashed it over my face. The water was warm. Uganda is truly a pearl!

Ben and I were jumping from rock to rock and enjoying the warmth of the mist. Sue took a few pictures, turned and yelled, "I'm going back to join the others."

I yelled back, "Okay, but blow that whistle if you run into any trouble."

She answered, "Okay, I'm on my way. See you back at the car.

All of a sudden, Ben, holding a heavy stick, jumped from rock to rock towards me and said, "Bwana Cuba, stay very still. There's a spider dangling from a tree branch. It's inflating its body and it's only two rocks behind you. Stay very still, Bwana. Very still."

Ben quickly brushed by me. "Whack! Whack! Whirl! Ben's pole struck, then threw the big spider towards the water in front of me.

As it was going by, I ducked. It nicked the hairline in the back part of my head.

Ben said, "Don't worry Bwana Cuba. Keep on your feet. Just go back the same way you came. I will be with you all the way. That spider is no more. You are safe."

Clutching the nape of my neck, I said, "That thing bit me on the neck. It feels like my shoulders are swelling up like I was a 'juiced-up' football lineman."

Ben said, "It's only an insect bite. Any poisonous swelling will subside within a day or so. Don't worry, Bwana Cuba. You are big and strong."

I thought: When the poison subsides? Easy for you to take it so lightly.

When we got back to the trail, I said, "What kind of spider was it? Poisonous? What do you say back there, Ben?"

"It was an aggressive one, I believe, Bwana Cuba. It may be poisonous, but not nearly as bad poisonous as a nykoa (snake) bite. A big man like you will survive."

I recalled the frightening story Harold Barker's 21 year-old daughter Patty, had told us a month ago.

She was bicycling, and a snake chased and nearly caught up to her. She believed it was that olive green snake with the black mouth—the black mamba whose poison is so quick acting its nickname is, "the eight-second mamba."

Snakes are either poisonous or constricting in Uganda.

The trip back to the cars was at record pace.

I said nothing to the others about the spider bite.

We're heading to Semliki to see the apes and baboons, then on to the Pygmies.

SAFARI 30

The journey to Semliki provided a rollicking good time, as the shocks and springs in the cars were tested to the limit. We arrived in good spirits, in spite of a rainstorm.

Our accommodations were a thing to behold: canvas tents with long, dark tree poles thatched over them tightly so that, supposedly, even a 400 pound gorilla couldn't visit us in our beds during the night.

Semliki smelled of danger!

It was right in the middle of an animal pathway to the nearby stream and we were told that during the night many wild animals in the region saunter through the camp. This is while we are trying our best to settle down to a night's rest?

Everything was outside, including the accommodation, loo (lavatory) and shower stalls, eating tables, chairs while some food was kept inside tightened down buckets and the rest hung in the trees.

This was camping like no other camping we'd experienced before. I believe we were one of the last groups to use these facilities before the fighting armies of Zaire and other countries took over the site.

My nostrils exploded with strange, pungent smells of a thatched-in jungle with little light and lots of eyes watching our every move.

Ben took us out on a trek to see the mountain gorillas but all we saw were hundreds of monkeys and fifty baboons. Ben warned all of us, "These creatures bite off the fingers of children who hold their fingers out to them. Don't ever stick your hands out to these animals."

My mind kept wandering, as I kept thinking that calling a group of baboons a parliament was wrong.

The nose and bum-picking Baboons are the loudest, most obnoxious, most viscously aggressive and least intelligent of all the primates.

All the children obeyed the Baboon warning, as they thoroughly enjoyed the antics of the swinging monkeys. Grunts and squeals filled the air and sometimes I thought the kid's voices were louder than the animals. Hilarity ruled.

Ben seemed shy and spoke with a slow, low pitch. He was well groomed.

We all found him to be an approachable person. He wore western style clothes and could dubbed a "neat freak:"—Everything in its place.

Ben and everyone were tired upon returning to the camp. After two hours rest, we were offered barbequed 'bush' meat, that we declined in favor of the fruits and vegetables that were on the table in the plenty. We had seen the flies around the meat.

Then to bed, and I guarded the entrance of our tent, between the canvas and the wooden poles overhang. With a heavy stick in hand, I don't recall sleeping a wink that night.

The night was filed with the sounds of a stampede of "clip-clops," from cloven-hoofed animals fleeing from "growling" big cats whose shadows I made out on the canvas, by the light of the full moon.

My imagination went wild, as I glanced over at the rest of the sleeping bodies in our tent. They are all out of it. I figure one grows used to noise. Like background music.

Africa is a noisy place! The African nights are nosier than Los Angeles traffic.

Suddenly, violent jerks moved the wood stacked on the side of the tent. What the heck is doing that? Then, I heard a groveled bark.

It's one of those slink-ended animals:—those, those, hyenas. They are mainly scavengers after a 'kill.' That 'kill' isn't going to be any of us.

I didn't want to yell, in case of wakening the others. I had my heavy stick raised and ready for action.

Any laughing jokester has to try getting by me. He'd be dead meat!

The stench emitted by the rascal was gagging me. Our tent was right under the wooden part of the roof the hyena was swaying from. By the light of the moon, I could see his distorted shadow on the tent. He even had a hump in his back like the humpback of Notre Dame, Quasimodo.

"Thump, thump, thump", followed by "boom, boom, and boom!"

Now what the . . . ? This sound is going to wake up everybody. I don't know how one can sleep in this din.

What is bashing those boards?

"CRACK! Thud! Ooh. Aah."

Did I hear one of our overhead stakes just crack and fall?

What the heck is that? It isn't laughing boy anymore.

It smells rotten and sounded almost human. Whatever it is, it's going to break down all our wooden top if it continues snapping boards up there.

Should I wake everyone to warn everyone as to where this thing is? Should I or shouldn't I? Crazy!

What the hell have you got your family into, Leo? What are you . . . ?

The tent moved. There was another loud crack and the canvas part of the tent flared up like a balloon and then settled. Has it gone?

"Thump, Thump, Thump," then a "Pal Lop, Pal Lop," followed by a "Pitter-Patter, Pitter-Patter," then golden silence.

I wonder if that was a??? Oh, no! Probably not! Probably those damn monkeys or dirty baboons that like to chew kids' fingers off. In the morning, I'll describe it, and then ask Ben what he thinks it was.

Jeez, my watch says it's five am already. I wonder what Bob thinks? Maybe not. He's at least two hundred yards away, in that safer spot he picked out for his tent.

It's getting light outside. These African nights are scary. I better put on a clean shirt and get some coffee going, that's if they have any here. Probably tea. Yeah, that'll do. There's a big difference between an African night and day.

Africa is a lot scarier at night, because it is in the darkness, when there's so much hunting and seeking going on. A person should own a camera that can take pictures during the night. I'm sure someone has probably already invented one.

In the morning, every adult yearned for a coffee and every kid dreamed to be waited on. The shower and the loo (toilet) drew line-ups.

I had asked Sue, "How did you sleep?

"Like a log."

"What about the kids?"

"Oh, they slept right through the night too. Why?"

"Oh, I just thought maybe you had heard something during the night."

"No, dear. It was just another uneventful night."

I queried others about last night and their replies varied from Flo's, "Oh, Bob snored too loud," to Bob's "You'll have to get used to noise in Africa. It's a known thing the indigenous can't be anything but noisy, even when I'm shooting a prized animal. Noise and Africa go together like fleas on a dog."

Daughter Laura said, "I was too bushed to hear anything, Dad."

"Ben, oh Ben, can I ask you a question? Do you think our Semliki Camp was visited by some strange animal's last night? If so, what?"

"Why do you ask, Bwana Cuba?"

"Come over here and look at these broken poles and these footprints, in the mud. What do you think was here last night?"

With a smile on his face, Ben answered, "Oh, Bwana Cuba, it appears that you were visited by one of the big apes. Hmm. Yes, oh yes! Yes, these could be the footprints of a big Silverback!"

"Can we go out and get some pictures of him today? What do you say to that, Ben? What do you say?"

Ben said, "I think no, Bwana Cuba. There is an army, fighting with guns and booming, just ten miles away from here and it is not safe to go on that safari today. We would be better leave here very soon and to go to the Pygmy camp today."

We broke camp, packed our cars and Ben led us further up the jerky trail.

I'll never forget that Semliki Camp.

A reliable source said, "That spot was never again a tourist camp. So many different armies had used it and still do today. A war is always going on in what used to be Zaire. It seems to never end and millions of innocent people have been killed."

CHAPTER SIX
ZAIRE HAD PYGMY PEARLS

SAFARI 31

After traveling some distance, suddenly many tiny people jumped onto the top of our car and clinging to the roof racks, started rocking it sideways, while yelling, "We are the Pygmies! We are the Pygmies!"

The sight of Sue and Laura's long blond hair sent the little people into hysterics. When they saw the two three-year old towheads in the back of our Volkswagen, they screamed with laughter. I'm glad all the kids were locked inside our car.

Possibly, this was the first time the pygmies had seen so much blond hair.

There must have been 40 or more pygmies. I noted that some had bows and arrows. Bob said, "I believe in there should be a new African saying:—The bullet is stronger than the ballot, but a gun without bullets kills nothing."

Ben, with his heavy mahogany stick, got out first and was swarmed, by a large group of small dancing people. We had given Ben our monies and he dealt half the charge to the Chief Katanga and displayed the rest in the air on its way to his pocket.

Chief Katanga was a typical male, Twa Pygmy of the Ituri Forest. He was just less than five feet tall and weighed no more than 80 lbs. The top of his head came up to the top part of my stomach (I'm six foot, three inches tall).

He wore a little whistle around his neck. The whistle, hanging on his tattered shirt, was used to keep track of other pygmies when hunting. His pigment was a light brown, due to how he lived in this dense jungle.

The typical females were topless. Chief Katanga's wife, Momma Musty stood four-feet, eight-inches. The top of her head came up to my belly button. She weighed 50 lbs. Her skirt was ragged and drab. When she smiled many missing teeth were revealed.

The tiny, curly haired, nude children had runny noses and protruding stomachs, signifying extreme malnutrition.

I thought: These people seem so happy and they appear to have so little. They are remnants of the hunter-gatherers of a long-ago Africa.

Ben had the tribe form a semi-circle to barter with us for their wares. One fellow wanted 50 shillings for the skin of an Okapi (Jungle giraffe) he had shot. Unfortunately, it hadn't been cured properly and was worth little.

Most of the playing instruments and carvings were bought up and the pygmies screamed when they made a sale. They were like little kids at a Sunday matinee.

The glassy-eyed, Chief Katanga had a perfectly muscled body. He was crouched with a spear behind the roots of a fig tree. Suddenly he joined the group, and staggered after Sue. He kept trying to sell her something strong than marijuana, in the pipe he was smoking.

Sue kept refusing his offer very diplomatically.

An elderly Pygmy, named Mau-Mau made up a lean-to so Chief Katanga could lean on it and smoke to his delight. He kept yelping like a puppy. I didn't know why he was making these sounds. Perhaps the powerful drugs he was smoking?

While everyone was focused on the Chief and his smoking, I noted the shanty hut with a radio hanging on the outside pole. The "boom-box" seemed out of place.

I said, "What's the Chief smoking, Ben?"

"Opium," was his answer.

"Is that what he was trying to sell to my wife?" "Yes, Bwana Cuba."

"What are the other weed-like, green things in the hands of that guy over there?"

"Oh, that's just Hashish, Bwana Cuba."

"Are these guys going to get out of control"?

"No. I don't think so, Bwana Cuba. They just like a good time."

I wondered if they were on drugs when the Germans visited?

Ben explained how the pygmies form a hunting party. "The women start it off, by making noise with their pots and pans, to drive the game, usually a small antelope, likely a blue duiker, into the net that's been set. Then, the men kill the animal, with their bows and with their pangas:—cut and skin it."

They then transport it to a neighboring town and exchange the meat for vegetables, grains and other things they want in their interdependent relationship. They use barter to get a balanced meal and survive.

"Why don't they grow the vegetables themselves?" I asked.

Ben said, "Oh, they are more hunters than farmers. The land where they live is not fertile for growing the vegetables they fancy. Besides, they don't make the time."

The women provided the logs for a fire, along with the knives, two pots and a basket. They had pulled saplings from the assembled shelters (endue). Each shack housed a single family. The walls were made of small, dark green monogongo leaves, mud and string.

The pygmies love their honey:—warm, musky, with the distilled sunlight and nectar of the tropical flower.

Life was motion to the pygmies. They lived to be fluid and free. Their living accommodations were portable, as is their camp.

Chief Katanga said, "We seem to be forever on the move."

I asked, "Why?"

"Because we are hunted by Zaire's army men who want to eat us."

Ben said, "It is because they (the troops) want to eat the pygmy so that they can absorb their good vision, bravery, hunting skills, toughness, ability to withstand a great deal of pain and dawa (magical powers). Pygmies are thought to be subhuman. Eating a pygmy is a goal for many of the Zaire militia."

I thought:—That's strange. The troops want the pygmies superior skills, even though they consider the pygmies less than human.

Violence begets violence.

The pygmies didn't fear death. For us, Chief Katanga fired up his pipe, leaned back, smoked till his eyes glowed, then sang their song of the dead:

"There's darkness upon us.

Darkness all 'round;

There's no light.

But, it is the darkness of the forest,

So if it really must be;

Even darkness is good."

I look around, with surprise, to see the forest suddenly electric white: suffused with the calm, almost glacial cleanliness of fluorescent lights of offices. A few yards away, the jungle turned metallic.

Falling rain, leaf shadows, the bloodied pelt of an arrowed monkey:—all appeared dipping, in silvery tones. There was a kaleidoscopic richness of light:—ethereal, hallucinating, filtering, as through an antique glass, unlike any other I'd ever seen before. It was beautiful!

Maybe some smoke drifting our way had caused it.

"I think it's time we leave, Ben," I said.

With that, we got back into our vehicles and left while the Twa Pygmies of the Ituri Forest waved and sang.

Chief Katanga said, "Come again and visit with us. You will always be welcome, Bwana Cuba."

They all seemed to be so happy.

Still, I felt relieved that we had left the Twa Pygmies before they overreacted to the hallucinatory drugs they were on.

I had noted how the female pygmies had blotched their bodies with paint, the eerie sounds of their flute becoming higher pitched, while the male pygmies had started clamoring and clawing for, "More shillingi." "More shillingi."

Ben guided us back down the trail to the Ugandan customs office at Mponawe, where he received his guide fee:—as well as a big hug and handsome cash bonus from me.

Bob said, "You be the big spender, Leo. I'm saving for another hunting safari in Tanzania."

"SUE AND GROUP OF ZAIRE'S TWA PYGMIES,
OF THE ITURI RAINFOREST."

"A HAPPY GANG OF ZAIRE'S TWA PYGMIES,
OF THE ITURI RAINFOREST."

CHAPTER SEVEN
GAME PARK PEARLS AD POISONS

SAFARI 32

We met our new Safari Guide, Tom Rigiwa, a 6'5" (Wa)Tutsi from neighboring Rwanda. Tom reminded me of a similar sized athlete/actor, Woody Strode, who had played professional football in the USA and Canada, before being cast as an African Maasai King in the movie, "King Solomon Mines."

I remembered Woody when he played for the 1948 Calgary Stampeders and how he helped coach the Central High School Rams where I played the same position he did—offensive end. Woody was a great teacher:—a real good listener and director.

Besides being a whole foot taller than Ben. Tom didn't possess a flat nose—the distinguishing mark of the Hutu tribe. Tom wore a large, tan Stetson hat, a khaki top and short pants with long, wool socks, inside his size 15 boots.

I asked, "Why do you wear your socks to up over your knees?

"So that a snake's bite cannot pierce my skin, Bwana, Cuba."

"When we get inside the Queen Elizabeth National Game Park gates, can we drive on the Equator Road to the Equator Landmark?" I asked Tom. "I'd also like you to take our family photo?"

"I will, if it doesn't take more than fifteen minutes, Bwana Cuba."

We drove through the tollgates, to the Equator Landmark and posed inside the tall, circular copper ring, on the white cement base, with a large N on the topside and a large S on the bottom. It was a temperate, blue-sky day, backed by the snow-capped Mountains of the Moon.

As we were driving towards the Park Lodge, Tom said, "This Park is famous for its tree-climbing lions. It's the only place in Uganda you will find these creatures. They are usually sleeping in a fig tree."

Sue asked, "Why is that?"

"Because they want to. Nothing more, Memsahib (European married lady)."

I interjected, "It's much too early to go to the Lodge. Why don't we take a day safari and try to capture this unusual site?"

With a scowl on his face, Tom said, "I think that we should take only one car, with adults only. The Peugeot will handle the park's rough terrain and the children's noise distractions could cause problems viewing tree-climbing lions."

After discussing it, we decided that Flo and her mother, with Laura's help, would look after the two towheads, at the Lodge. Bob would drive his Peugeot, while Ton would navigate by Bob and Sue and I were in the back seat. We would go on a day safari to see and take pictures of the tree-climbing lions.

Bob drove on the main road for about ten miles, then Tom said, "Let me get out and walk in the field over yonder to view animal spoor. I will guide you to 'the King of Beasts.' These lions are special. They appear to be gentle and slow, but they can quickly spring like no other animal can."

Tom took long strides ahead of us. We drove at 15 to 20 M.P.H. over the four feet high anthills and deep ditches to keep us. Bob's car drove like a truck in that flexible springs were lacking. I hit my head, more than ten times on the ceiling. Nearly a K.O.! Sue held onto my arm with a tight grip. I thought, Hey! It was like we were a-rockin' and a-rollin' on a bronc, at the Calgary Stampede:—"The Biggest Outdoor Show on Earth."

Tom put his hand up like an Indian scout, jumped in the car and said, "Bwana Bob, drive as fast as you can over the savanna in an easterly direction. Turn right when we get to the Hippo pools, then stop."

With Bob's foot heavy on the gas pedal, the French-made car made like a Sherman tank leaving billows of sand dust that could be seen for miles. Ground hogs, with tails up, and squirrels scattered as well as lots of unrecognizable birds.

I thought: what's the big hurry? At this rate, we're going to have an accident.

I said, "Hey, Bob:—Don't you think we're going a little too fast?"

"You want to see the tree-climbing lions today?"

"Yes, but I don't want to die doing it."

Tom piped in, "This fast way you will be able to see them, Bwana Cuba"

"I still think we're going too fast for safety's sake, Tom. There's no use us getting in a car accident. There's always tomorrow."

Bob cut in, "Yes, I think you may be right Leo, but Tom's the guide, not you. He knows what we have to do to see these wonders."

Just then, the Peugeot became airborne and crashed down into a ditch, with Bob's and Tom's heads hitting the front window. The driver's door flung open and Bob fell out the door just as I spied the leaping lion.

"Bob! Lion! Lion! Get back in the car!"

Somehow, Tom leapt sideways, out the open door, grabbed Bob's arm, swung him back into the driver's seat while jumping in over him and closing the door with his foot as the giant cat hit the driver's door of the rocking car. Sue and I were both yelling, "Get in! Close the door! Get in and close . . . Whew! What a close call!"

Tom said sternly to a shaking Bob, "Never get out of your car, Bwana Bob! Never! Never! They will eat you! I can't shoot them! I have no bullets!"

I took over the driving while Sue put a blanket over Bob, who was in the back.

When I looked outside, there were four lions circling our vehicle.

I said, "Are these the tree-climbing lions you're guiding us to, Tom?"

"These four are her cubs. She's slumbering over to the west, in that fig tree, about 100 yards away. See her?"

"How do you know those four are just cubs? That one sprang about 40 feet to nearly get Bob and you."

"See the spots on their bellies? That shows they're just cubs. Their mother's a full-grown, tree-climbing lion. Take your pictures from the car. Stay in the car. You don't want to be dinner for the Queen and her family."

I thought: This Tom sure speaks his mind, doesn't he? He's no Ben. Bob didn't purposely end up out of the car. It was the force of that jolt after hitting the ditch at such high speed. Speed kills!

We got some good pictures. I took a couple good pictures for Bob, backed the smoking Peugeot out of the ditch, put it in gear and slowly drove on, without hitting the snarling, wide-mouthed carnivores. I thought: Bye kitties. Go climb a tree!

Bob sobbed, "Please don't tell my family. They think of me as 'the Great White Hunter.' It'd devastate them to see me here crying and shaking. Drive back slowly so I can get myself composed, Leo. Okay?"

"Sure thing, Buddy. Not a word to the others. We'll take the slow road home like we're on a slow boat to China." I started to hum that tune that was made popular by Jo Stafford.

By the time we got back to the camp, the red flames from campfire were spiraling in the air, and the gals had prepared a good supper for us, "tree climbing lion explorers." We were treated like royalty. The Ngege (Tilapia fish) was a very tasty dish; the ladies had bought from the lodge.

We talked about our pictures of the lioness in the fig tree; how she snored as we took her picture and the spots on her cubs and how many bumps we had to absorb to get those pictures. They'd better turn out.

Flo said, "Maybe tomorrow, you guys could go fishing in one of the many lakes here. That way, you won't come home so late and tired."

I thought: Oh Flo, if you only knew how close you were to becoming a widow you wouldn't let Bob out even on a lake in this Game Park.

We went to bed early that evening, without a clear picture of tomorrow.

SAFARI 33

The night before, at supper, Tom had recited off a long list of the flora and fauna we could see in the Queen E. tomorrow. Instead of inspiring us, it had made us sleepy; thus the early bedtime.

Before turning in I asked him, "Are there any snakes in this Park?"

Tom said, "Oh yes, Bwana Cuba. Uganda has 400 types of snakes."

"Are they all poisonous?"

"No, some don't destroy life, Bwana."

"Are our tents, snake-proof?"

Yes, Bwana. The askaris' (guards') will be protecting your tent all night long. No snakes for you, Bwana. No 'creepies'! Funny, eh?"

"You're hilarious, Tom."

I thought: What a strange guy. He thinks I'm a chicken. I wonder how many times he's been bitten?

We were up with the throng of melodious birds at red-dawn and got the fire flaming; breakfast on and over.

Bob's crew was just getting up as we were finished off our coffee.

I said, "Hey, Buddy are 'youse' guys ready to rock 'n roll?"

"No, we'll let you go ahead. We're going to stay around the Lodge."

"Any reason?"

"Oh, Flo's not feeling well this morning. She needs her rest."

Sue said, "Let me drive, Leo. You need a break. You'll be the navigator today. I'll operate the V.W. 'pole-pole' (slowly, slowly) on the tarmac roads today. You can take the pictures, with my consultations."

"Okay, I'll go get Tom. He can sit in the back with the kids or walk out front of the car, if he wants to."

Bob piped up, "Oh, our guide, Tom left late last night. He woke me up and said that he'd pulled a leg muscle and was getting a ride back south. I settled with him. Here's his bill. You owe me your half. Want to settle up now?"

"Yes, here's my 700 shillings. He charges more than Ben doesn't he? I thought they had the same per diem rate. Guess not."

Sue said, "I've bought a Queen E. government road map in Kampala. Here it is. Let's leave the Lake Edward's portion and head up the Kazinga channel to Lake George. Maybe, as a family, we'll see a tree-climbing lion and some elephants. Tom told me the elephants here are quite different from the ones we'll see in the Murchison Game Park.

"How so?"

"They're a runty size. Seems they've been crossed with the Congo elephant, so they're not as big as the East African Bush Elephant, that's so popular in Uganda."

Queen Elizabeth Game Park is in the great lakes and savanna region (grassland dotted, more or less, with trees and bushes). You can look for miles and miles before you reach the distant animals, without fences and the open sky go on forever and ever.

On our Day Safari, we nicknamed our Volkswagen Fastback, "Yellow Bee' and saw many signs saying:—"ELEPHANTS HAVE THE RIGHT OF WAY."

We kept an eye out for "the big huskers" and tree-climbing lions.

I thought: Elephants are creatures of habit. It's up to humans to figure out how to co-exist with them in these shared spaces. From what I've heard and read, elephants and humans have laid routes all across Uganda and many of them crisscross one another.

Uganda resembles a black pearl—never colonized like Kenya and many other African countries—in the middle of a bulging sandwich, which is the continent, Africa.

We saw three warthogs (daddy, mommy and baby); a herd of twenty Topi (looked a lot like our mountain goat); one unloved spotted hyena scavenging off antelope bones; a fine males Bushbuck with a Waterbuck and a Hartebeest and five Egyptian Geese; a herd of twenty Uganda Kob (local antelope)—the emblem of Uganda's

National Parks; a black and red Ground Hornbill bird; a Saddle-Bill Stork; a Tufted Guinea fowl like our turkey;) mini-Buffalo Egrets and yes, one tree-climbing lion.

Sue took over the camera and got great pictures of all of these animals.

It was nearing dusk, as we were traveling on our way back to camp, just after the Kazinga channel into Lake Edward, when I spied them and shouted, "Hey, Sue there's over a hundred Cape Buffaloes that are going to cut-across the road for the lake right through us. See."

Two Scout Buffaloes, with white egret birds on their back, were menacing the front fenders of our car. A massive herd was right behind them. Sue took a picture of them. Then, they started to trot towards us and accelerated their speed.

I yelled, "Kids hit the floor. Gun it, Sue"

Ding! Wham! Both front fenders folded in like an accordion causing a sudden stoppage.

"Hit the gas, gal."

Bam! Smash! A ping off the windshield caused it to crack in a jagged line.

"Gun it!"

Crunch! Wham! There went a dent in the passenger side and back door.

"Go to the left flank."

Swish! Swoosh! We were suddenly smooth and clear.

"Right now, Sue, floor it. For God's sake, gun it!"

"Go gal! Go! Don't stop!

The reddish-brown Buffaloes had bunted, bumped and bruised our "Yellow Bee," but we had miraculously survived.

Sue had saved the day by her "dipsy-doodle" driving and "putting meddle to the pedal," at the right time and "the pedal down to the medal," when the opening occurred.'

Wide-eyed, Sue had zigzagged through narrow openings left by the snorting, mass-horned, red-eyed beasts, while nearly running over a calf then clear, flat land ahead.

It was a driving exhibition that an African Safari road-race driver would have been envious of.

Sweat kept pouring off our faces and backs, as we seemed to have been looking at certain death. What a driver, Sue is. My Gal can sure drive!

"'You can slow down now, Sue. They're all gone. You've done it! Thank God. No need to speed. Go pole-pole (slowly-slowly), all the way back to camp, please."

There was no way that Sue would let up on the pedal and we made it back to camp and Lodge in record time.

A chilly Lodge Manager, Mr. Singh greeted me with, "Bwana Jacques, your car's driving much too fast for our roads. You will have to drive 'pole-pole' because, don't forget:—'ELEPHANTS HAVE THE RIGHT OF WAY.' We don't want you and your family to be in an accident, Bwana Jacques."

I asked Singh, "Where are the Zachs?"

He handed me a note. It read, "Jacques: We pushed off for Murchison Falls Game Park. Flo isn't feeling so well. See ya all there. Bob"

We decided to stay the night in our tent at Queen E. and push on, next morning, after breakfast, for Murchison.

Our tee-ny bopper daughter, Laura was complaining about being bitten on her arm by a fly. The bite had drawn blood. Sue gave her some antibiotic salve to put on it. By the next morning, the arm was swollen up.

Sue asked Mr. Singh, "Can you look at it?"

He examined and said, "Oh my! Oh my! It may be she was bitten by tsetse fly. Can I ask her some questions?"

He asked Laura, "Miss Jacques, could you please be so kind as to describe this fly that bit you? What color was it?"

Laura said, "I didn't really get a really good look at it, but it was about the size of a . . . oh a . . . horse fly, and . . . yes, it was brown in color."

"Were its wings folded like scissors down its back?"

"Yes, I think they were."

Mr. Singh swung around and said to Sue and said, "Hmm, I think you better get a doctor to look at her arm just to make sure it's not a tsetse fly bite. Tsetse flies cause sleeping sickness. Sometimes it's fatal."

He went on to tell us that between 1898 and 1915 a particularly lethal strain of sleeping sickness had wiped out all the equine animals, such as zebras, and killed, then driven, the remaining humans and their livestock out of the areas now occupied by the two big game parks, Queen Elizabeth and Murchison Falls, as well as most Northwestern areas.

Therefore, the animals with a built-in resistance to the sickness, flourished and roamed in something like their former splendor before man, with his gun hunter ways arrived. Hence, the wild animals had found an unexpected ally, unhappily though, it was a sinister one that even the staunchest conservationist wouldn't have wished for.

"Okay, we'll head pronto for the nearest hospital in Fort Portal."

"Oh no, Bwana Jacques. Fort Portal is 78 kilometers away. You are Canadians, are you not?"

"Yes, we're born and raised in Canada. We're proud Canadians!"

"Then, you go to Kilembe Mines. A Canadian company, Falconbridge Nickel, owns it. It's only a half-hour from here. They have their own Hospital. It is much better than the one in Fort Portal. It has better doctors and nursing staff and more up-to-date drugs. It's very close for you.

"Thank you, Mr. Singh. Is there anyone in particular we should ask for?"

"Yes, please ask for Dr. Patel. He's a good friend of mine and is the most skilled medical person in Uganda. He knows sleeping sicknesses symptoms and what must be done to combat the disease. Tell him I sent you, please. I think he knows of you Mr. Jacques."

I said, "Thank you again for all your help.

"LOOKING FOR TROUBLE:"—CAPE BUFFALO, THAT SURROUNDED OUR CAR, SCOUTING TO STAMPEDE.

Leo Louis Jacques

"BIG FELLAS"—HIPPO AND CROC, IN VICTORIA NILE RIVER

SAFARI 34

Sue lead-footed the 10 kilometers in record time. On the outskirts, we observed our first Ugandan "Western-style" Supermarket, on the main road sporting the eastward sign, "Kilembe mines five kilometers."

We were heading into the Mountains of the Moon once again. We passed the exclusive Margherita 18-hole golf course and past three exquisite estates on large acreages, before finally arriving at the Kilembe Mines Hospital.

Dr. Patel's receptionist greeted us with forms to fill out. Sue and Laura were quickly ushered into the doctor's examining room. After completing the forms, I followed them into the large room, where I met Dr. Patel.

The doctor greeted me, "Hello, Mr. Jacques. My brother, Jan is a fellow Rotarian with you at the Kampala club. He's told me many nice things about you and your challenging assignment. You have many admirers. I read, with interest, your bi-weekly newspaper column."

"Thank you, Dr. Patel. Please, have you looked at my little girl's arm? What do you think? Has she been bitten by the tsetse fly or not?"

"I think, possibly she has, but not to worry. I have a strong antibiotic that will certainly make short work of any sleeping sickness. Trust me! I know, you and your dear wife, fret about your child being bitten, but please, don't worry. We now have the answers to such problems."

"How much do I owe you?"

"It's on the house, or should I say, our Hospital, Mr. Jacques. It was a distinct honor to meet you. Please remember me and my brother, down the road."

I thought: What a nice man. What is he talking about—remembering him and his brother, down the road? Hmm.

"Thank you, so much, Dr. Patel. I'll tell Jan that we met and how you helped us. You have been too kind."

"I understand from your dear wife, Sue, you are on your way to Murchison. Here's my card. Phone me anytime. We are hooked up all over East Africa in more ways than one, if you get my meaning. Anytime, day or night for you and your family. I am your humble servant."

Sue said, "Could you please explain the instructions about the pills to my daughter, Dr. Patel. She's a curious tee-ny bopper and doesn't always listen, Doctor. Please, SPELL IT OUT FOR HER!"

Dr. Patel obliged. He asked Laura to repeat it back to him.

I thought: This guy would make a great teacher.

Before we hit the road, I asked, "Should we check into the hospital in Fort Portal at all?"

"Oh, Mr. Jacques. Please, don't question my judgment. Your daughter doesn't need to be checked by the doctors at Fort Portal. Instead, I would have them look at the swelling from the ugly bite you have in your back hairline. I think it is causing your back a lot of swelling and obvious discomfort. You will need surgery. Still, if I were you, I'd wait until you get back in Kampala. You should look up

Mr. Fletcher. He's a fine surgeon. The best in East Africa, if not all of Africa!"

Oops, I thought I'd hidden that bite. Why does he call a surgeon Mr.? Aren't the surgeons at Mulago Hospital doctors? (Note: Kampala's Mulago was a 1961 gift to Uganda from the British—it was then called, "Africa's best hospital.")

"Thank you, kind doctor. I will be sure to look up Dr. Fletcher."

"Yes, Mr. Jacques, but please don't call him Dr. Fletcher. British surgeons are called Mister not Doctor. It's the British way! Thank you."

Wow, learn a new thing every day.

On the way out of Kilembe, I stopped at the large Kilembe Recreation Hall and treated our family to British Whimpy Burgers. It was the first meat we had eaten since the Lake Victoria Hotel's roast pig dinner.

Even though these burgers didn't stack up against A. & W.'s, they were a most welcome change from all the fish, fruit and vegetables we'd been eating.

I'd lost close to 20 lbs. since coming to Uganda. I was now a middleweight—not a 'light heavy.' Continuing of a non-meat diet will make me a welterweight, again and I may consider a comeback.

Kilembe Mines is a company town of 7,000. The top men are Canadians, with the middle management made up of white South Africans and 6,000 black, Ugandan Indigenous workers, whose first names only were on the salary list.

Why? So their extended family would not know that they were earning any income and consequently want a share. Yes, East African Socialism, all over again.

Top and middle management executives lived in exquisite, estate-like houses on acreages, whereas the indigenous lived in single-room junior quarters with outdoor plumbing.

The modern-looking Supermarket sold foodstuffs, sugar, soap, and other items, such as liquor, on credit:—With deductions from the Indigenous man's monthly wages.

The saying around Kilembe Mines was, "If there is money and liquor, sex is never far away." In a nearby town, there was a stable of street walking and willing prostitutes, available for the administration and the miners.

We passed by Fort Portal and the many tea estates on one side of the road and coffee estates on the other. On the hilltop was the Palace of the Mukawa, the hereditary ruler of the Kingdom of Toro.

Toro is known for its large women. The Toro ladies of rank are allowed to take no exercise and are forcibly fed food and milk till they reach an enormous size.

Fort Portal has many coffee and tea plantations with the mist-shrouded Mountains of the Moon as a backdrop.

We joined a family of eight for a meal of the mashed plantations called mutoke seeping groundnut oil. These people were warm, with happy, healthy children in scenic landscaping

Both our kids were chiming, "When do we get to the Game Park?"

Sue answered, "We're going to stop off and visit with the Sams in Masindi. It's only 88 kilometers from our destined campground at Paara Lodge in Murchison."

Wally and Nona Sam, with their two girls, Lara and Marnie, were a welcome sight to behold. Wally asked us adults to a going away party for two young British teachers who'd worked eighteen months straight and was now going on a six-month holiday before going home.

The party was held at Bob and Marianne MacLeod's place. Laura babysat Lara, Marnie and KC at Sam's place.

At the party, loud African music filled the air. The two guests of honor had brought the wife of Uganda's Minister to Israel with them.

Her name was Rose. She was of the Bugandan tribe and wore the traditional, many-layered, bright Babushka dress. Her face perspired throughout the evening.

Her manner was soft-spoken and shy.

I asked, "Your husband is in Tel Aviv right now?"

"Yes. He is finishing his pilot's license and learning about new armaments."

I questioned, "What was Israel's role, if any, in the forming of the 2nd Republic of Uganda?"

"Oh, it was the Israelis who made the plan to put President Amin in power. They were mad at former President Obote for supporting the Sudanese whom the Jews were fighting."

I said, "I thought it was the British who had been the main country helping Amin in removing Obote from power in Uganda.

"No, that is wrong. The Israelis were the main plotters for the ousting of Obote so that General . . . I mean . . . President Amin could take power."

We made small talk about her husband's important post; her children; her family; the Buganda tribe and other aspects of tribalism and East African Socialism in Uganda.

I enjoyed conversing with Rose.

The two Englishmen, Mark and Thomas got drunk on Waragi, the cheap Ugandan whiskey and were worn out by dancing with every woman in the place.

Finally, we pushed the two of them into the back of their jeep and one of the other guests; Doug Abram drove them and Rose to their residences.

Sue and I enjoyed the evening and caught up on what was going on around Masindi and how the Sams were coping with their new experiences.

Wally presented me with a valise that he'd made from the skin of a 22-foot python.

Five Ugandans Indigenous tribesmen had brought him the live snake in a bag and had asked if Wally was interested in buying it.

The men brought the python snake out of the bag and held it firmly as Wallie inspected it. They wanted seven shillings (one dollar) a foot for it, but after much 'dickering,' settled for four shillings a foot.

Following the 88-shilling purchase of the python snake, it was put back in the bag and then speared it to death. There were sewing marks all over the valise.

The friendly town of Masindi is a pleasant stopover, on your way to Murchison Falls for a boat trip, up the Victoria Nile, surrounded by hippos and long crocodiles.

The next morning we pushed off for the Murchison Game Park. We set up camp at the campground near Paara Lodge. The Zachs were residing in the Lodge. We all booked a boat trip on the Victoria Nile up to Murchison Falls and back. There were so many bookings that three 20-people boats were necessary.

The river was dark and fast flowing with many birds flying over and around us. We saw long crocodiles over 20 feet and groups of hippos swimming and diving.

Our helmsman Herb said, "We have to be very wary of the hippo as it has overturned and killed many people. It can even overturn this forty-foot boat. The hippo kills more people than any other animal in Uganda."

I thought: They sure have big mouths with vicious looking teeth. Not to be fooled with, that's for sure.

Herb drove the boat right up on shore beside a sleeping 20-foot crocodile and said, "There you are. Take some close-ups of this fellow."

Sue leaned over and took an eye-to-eye shot of the crocodile, just as it was opening its eyes. What a close-up picture that was!

Herb put the boat in reverse and the engines roared. We proceeded down the dark river till we saw a giant bull elephant, with a huge white identifying spot on his side, in the water. He'd broken off part of the shore and was devouring the grass in his trunk. We noticed a big white circle on his one side, which Herb explained was put there by the game warden to warn of a dangerous rogue elephant.

I asked Herb, "What is that mark on the side of the elephant?"

"Oh, that's just some dye the warden put on him to show that he's a rogue elephant who is dangerous to be close to. We will steer clear of him."

And so our journey continued on the magnificent Victoria Nile River. Ahead of us were the falls that I had only seen in the movies and had heard excelled Niagara Falls.

SAFARI 35

Murchison Falls is one of the natural wonders of the world.

The Victoria Nile has its origin at Jinja, where it leaves Lake Victoria. After 50 miles it passes through the swamps of Lake Kyoga and flows another 200 miles before it enters the northeast corner of Lake Albert.

By the time it enters Lake Albert, it is already a great river. Yet:—and this is the incredible part—at Murchison Falls the whole, vast river is forced through a gorge less than 20 feet wide.

I recalled a movie where the bad (muzongu) white guy was fighting the good guy, African American, Jimmy Brown as they tumbled, tossed and tripped down a mighty gorge into the Victoria Nile. They had been washed over beautiful Murchison Falls. What a struggle it was! Jimmy Brown won the fight and was the hero of the show.

When we arrived at the bottom of the falls, Herb offered to pull the boat over and let us out to climb to the top of the falls. He got the helmsman from the Zach's boat to do the same. All of us climbed up the 150-foot trail to the top of the falls.

Along the trail we met a group of five men who scurried past us as they came down toward to the shoreline. They ignored our greetings, had long pangas (machetes) in their hands and kept their heads low down as though they didn't want to be recognized. We continued on our way up. When we arrived at the top, there were gentle breezes, accompanied by spray and mist from the water. It whipped our hair like a whirlwind from a whirlybird (helicopter).

We read the inscription etched in the stone monument on the ground.

It read, "Queen Victoria visited Murchison Falls and this bridge has been built in her honour, so she can go from one side to the other in order to enjoy the view.

This she did. As soon as she returned from the other side, to where you are standing, the bridge collapsed and was eroded by the river, never to be used again."

We hadn't heard this story before, nor have we heard it since.

From the top of Murchison Falls, we looked down onto the mighty Victoria Nile that was about a hundred yards wide and flowing swiftly between steep, scrub-covered banks about 200 feet high.

In the distance, we could see lake pools below "the Falls." A half-dozen hippos, with Cormorant birds standing on their backs, lay in the calmer water, further up the far side and a pair of fish eagles with snowy-white heads and black wings screaming and circling above the river.

The falls were spectacular and their rolling nature reminded me of the Bow Falls outside of Banff, Alberta:—where Marilyn Monroe and Robert Mitchum had starred in the movie, "River of No Return."

After Sue and Flo had their fill of taking in the scenery and snapping pictures, we descended to the edge of the Murchison Falls and stood on the rocks in the spray looking into the seething turmoil where the white water sped past and fell in a series of cataracts 400 feet to a great muddy pool below.

The mighty Victoria Nile flowing into Murchison Falls is one of the most remarkable and awe-inspiring sights I have ever seen.

We felt safe when we got to our boats. It was a limbering workout for all of us.

At the boat, Sue snapped a picture of four elephants:—Daddy, Mommy, Brother and Sister, having drank of the Nile, turning around, lifted their tails and ran into the jungle.

The first question I asked Herb was, "Did you see the group of scraggly looking men with the big pangas?"

"Yes, Bwana Cuba. They ran when they saw that I had spied them. They are poachers and I radioed the warden as to their whereabouts. We are always on the lookout for such bad men. These wicked men are killers of our Park's wildlife. Thank you Bwana Cuba for telling me. Do not worry yourselves about such evil men. They will be caught and exterminated like the vermin that they are."

With that violent and savage thought, our group sat subdued all the way back to Paara Lodge. We were worn out.

The memories of Murchison Falls are still emblazed in our memory banks. The poachers did bother me. I tried to think back to the times when I had caught a glimpse of a man's shirt while trekking in the bush. I had thought it was just my imagination and had dismissed it as that.

Further, we had no idea that so many hippos and crocodiles existed in Uganda, let alone in a few miles of the Victoria Nile.

When we got back to the campground, we visited the Zachs for an hour. Bob told me, "We'll be leaving for our home in the morning, so that I can bag a few more trophies as I've paid for the privilege in Tanzania. Uganda doesn't offer such a liberty."

Bob also mentioned that since they had arrived at Paara Lodge the "buzz" of the place concerned a British couple. They had set up a tent for their family, then left the five-year old girl and three-year old boy in the tent while they went to the Lodge bar for a drink and a nibble.

The nasty part of the whole experience was the two children wandered out of the tent and had tried to play with the baboons.

When the kids poked their fingers at the baboons, the animals grabbed their hands and ate off four of the five fingers on each youngster's right hand. The baboons had 'chawed' off each finger right down to the knuckle. What a painful experience for those two unfortunate youngsters!

The bar-drinking parent's guilt evidently showed, as well.

That evening, we had a tasty fish supper around the campfire behind the Lodge, chatting with a German geologist named Hans who said he had many interesting stories to tell about Uganda.

I asked the handsome, thirty-something, blond-haired, blue-eyed Hans, "Do you have any non-terrifying stories?'

"Yes. I had such an encounter with a spitting creature."

"A spitting creature?"

Hans said, "Well, it was just about this time of the day, and as I wandered down by the Victoria Nile that I decided to have a dip in the river. By the light of a full August moon, jumped in where I thought it was safe. It was mighty dark. Still, the moon gave off enough light so that any crocodile eyes could easily be spotted."

He went on, "After a refreshing dip, I grabbed my towel that I'd left on a large rock. I was starting back to the camp, when I saw the image of a twisted shadow mirrored in the water and had wondered what it was. It proved to be a long snake that spits its venom. It's known as the Spitting Cobra. Its slimy stuff covered my back from top to bottom."

I asked, "What did you do?"

"I kept on walking briskly while wiping all the gunk off my back. I did this without turning my head. I knew that I had no cuts or bruises on my back and kept my eyes frontward at all times in case the serpent reloaded and shot another barrage at me."

I said, "That's quite a story. I didn't even know there was such a snake as a Spitting Cobra."

He answered, "There are actually four types of cobra snakes in Uganda. The largest and most lethal is the Egyptian Cobra that, along with the Spitting Cobra, is common in Murchison. This Spitting Cobra is sometimes called the Black-Necked Cobra.

The other two cobras are: the Black-Lipped Cobra and Gold's Forest Cobra. Those two are found only in the Queen Elizabeth Game Park."

An irate Sue interrupted the conversation with, "Enough! That's enough talk about such 'creepy-crawly' things. The children won't be able to sleep a wink tonight if they keep hearing such stories about snakes."

Hans said, "Sorry, Frau Jacques. My loving lips are sealed to any more talk of such things. You good-looking, dizzy blonds surely get red-faced when mad. Your nose curls when you speak your mind. You're a Frau with spirit! You Herr Jacques are very fortunate."

I said, "Yes, I am a happy man to have a gorgeous and intelligent wife. Sue's got a high I.Q., and also a high S.Q. (social quotient), that you, Hans seem to lack."

We slept well that night, and in the morning, decided to explore more of Murchison Falls. We spent most of the day pursuing two skyscraping, Rothschild Giraffe species around the Park. Sue loved the giraffes.

We also saw other animals such as warthogs, wild dogs, jackals, monkeys and baboons. Still, it was the giraffe eating the fruit off the tall sausage tree that stole the show. Yes, the brown fruit did indeed look like a sausage in color and length.

A dozen Marabou Stork strutted about, like old gents in white waistcoats. These revolting birds were carrion feeders like vultures and have hideous naked pouches at their throat where they store food.

I was startled when we went around a bush and were within 50 yards of a black rhino. I had heard that these snorting animals couldn't see well and charge without any hesitation. We quickly left his range.

Not far away from where we had met Mr. Rhino was the remnants of a dead rhino minus its tusks and legs. The poachers must have been there recently. From the car, we took close-up pictures of the remains of the rhino so we could give them to the game warden and explain where the body was. Why take the legs?

Rather than taking all the pictures from the safety of our vehicle, I decided to relieve Sue of the camera, get out of our Volkswagen and take a close-up. Something in my gut told me to step back in and quickly close the car door.

Instantly, there was a solid 'kpow' against the side of the car. It was another snake. I watched it slither off into the long, Nile grass.

I was lucky to have trusted my instincts that time.

Sue said, "Don't you think we've had a full enough day? Maybe we should get back to the campground."

"Sure thing, gorgeous." Surprising how it takes another man to make one appreciate one's mate even more.

That evening, we decided to leave Laura in charge of KC while we went and danced the evening away in the Lodge. The dance floor was full of stuffy Brits who seemed to have no appreciation for anything but the waltz.

We waltzed then jived, then did the tango, the rumba, the fox trot and even the boogie-woogie. It was a great evening of fun. The band was hip, with a great trumpet player. I thought:—These African bands are hot.

The next morning we saw 8 pelicans and four pairs of saddle-billed storks. Graceful cinnamon-and-white jacanas searched for food.

Among the trees in Murchison were a large number of Sausage Trees (Kigelia Ethiopica) with fruit resembling hanging cucumbers.

Our tent accommodation had the usual outdoor tent lavatory with a coldwater shower attached. Wooden reinforcements over the canvas of all the tents kept the baboons and hyenas outside.

The joys of not driving straight through village in safari vans heading for National Game Parks, but diverting to small villages and getting involved helps one understand the local people.

Our findings were much different from the expected images contrived from the media and tour guides. We feel we have a broader view of the country, while building strong and lasting relationships, and enhancing our humanity as well as benefiting the small, rural, local communities rather than the big city media blitz that ends up in the pockets of the rich Africans interest in only building skyscrapers in Kampala.

After a night's rest, we packed up and left for Kampala.

The kids were inquisitive about every living thing. We did our usual "sing-song" and African quiz/test, as a way of breaking the long trip. There were no "Golden Arches" on these tarred and dusty roads.

To us, African drivers often used their signal lights to tell you what to do. Furthermore, we had to make sure to dodge them when they drove from one side of the road to the other.

Many autos and lorries (trucks) were abandoned and left by the side of the road. Often they had just run out of petrol.

Sue did nearly all of the driving homeward. My exploding head, painful neck and back were throwing off my concentration.

When not driving, I went in and out of consciousness. I was quite sick.

Sue said, "As soon as we get back, you're going to Mulago Hospital and see that surgeon, Leo. You should never put off things like that."

She was right. Life's too short to be too little.

CHAPTER EIGHT
MEDICAL PEARLS AND POISONS

SAFARI 36

When we got back to our Uganda College compound, the first thing we did was have the house checked. Lucas and Onyango took our dog, Bonzo through the house to ensure there weren't any snakes. We still had our geckos on the wall and our sugar ants in the bathroom, but thankfully, no snakes or scorpions.

After getting the kids settled down, Sue drove me over to the Mulago Hospital. I asked for an appointment to see Mr. Fletcher concerning a large swelling on my neck that was affecting my concentration, mobility and spine.

The admitting nurse said, "Please fill out these forms. Dr. Ismali will be with you shortly. You must see him before he schedules any surgery for Mr. Fletcher. You say your name is Leo Jacques. Are you the same one who is in the newspaper nearly as much as our beloved President?"

"I guess, that's true. Any problem with that?"

"No Bwana Cuba. I think you have made quite an impression on many Ugandans. We need good men like you to educate our young."

After meeting briefly with Dr. Ismali, I was given many pills and shots to deaden the pain, while being admitted into a private room. A scheduled operation by Mr. Fletcher was set for eight a.m., next morning.

It was five a.m. when they started prepping me.

I met Mr. Fletcher at 7:45 a.m. He was a slim, balding, forty-something, blue-eyed man with an abrupt manner. Initially, he was devoid of any smiles or small talk. His manner was direct and terse. Then he spoke with a strong Scottish brogue.

"So, . . . you're the Canadian who's in the local news a spot. It seems that you're everywhere. Eek! Where-oh-where did you pick up this nasty gash, on your hair-line?"

"I think it was in the Mountains of the Moon area, Mr. Fletcher."

"You're not sure are you? Were you at all near Zaire?"

"Only on its edges, visiting the Twa Pygmies."

Mr. Fletcher said, "I'll bet you didn't know that Twa is the Scottish word for two? Furthermore, their proper name is not Twa Pygmies. They're properly known as, 'the Batwa, the wee inhabitants, of the Ituri Forest.'"

"No, Sir, I didn't. The Scotch surely do get around a lot."

Mr. Fletcher said, "Yes, we do. Now, Jacques, I'll give you my prognosis: Bitten by a highly venomous spider and, lad, you are fortunate to be alive. The spider's stinger must have struck against this bone in the back of you're head.

You now have a sack of poison and, bit-by-bit, it's been releasing itself into the rest of you're body and causing paralysis of you're lower extremities. You must be a bit daft to have forgone treatment of this until now. I think you're one favored 'booby.' Life could very easily be over for you. You must have someone watching over you."

I said, "What are you going to do about this . . . this poison, Mister Fletcher?"

Mr. Fletcher said, "Oh, a bit of a sharpness in you, Jacques. Well, that's a fine 'tado' for me trying to save your miserable life. So you best relax and let the stuff I've given you work its way through your thick hide and head and into your blood stream.

It'll neutralize the poison and patch you up. You'll take all of our hospital's blood supply for you to survive. Cheerio, Jacques. Count your blessings!"

I felt like I had a hole in the back of my now bandaged head. When I woke up, the room was spinning. I kept closing and re-opening my eyes.

I needed to focus on something. I fixed my eyes on a dark spot on the wall and, over and over and uttered to myself: I can do all things through God to be healthy.

I heard Surgeon Fletcher say, "Well, Jacques what do you think of living? Are you up to putting in another 18-hour day of work?"

I said, "Maybe tomorrow or the next day. What have you done to my head, Mister . . . Mister Fletcher?"

Mr. Fletcher said, "You're still coming out of the knockout stuff we had to use on you. We reverted back to ether. Didn't want anything to mix with all that poison in your system, Jacques. Besides being daft, you're one benign lad."

I said, "How long am I going to be in here? I've got to get back to work right away."

Mr. Fletcher said, "Oh, I can release you right now, if you press me buttons, Jacques. You just relax and let nature work its wonders. You don't have to save the world today. You heroes are all the same. Appreciate that you're alive, man."

"It's okay for you to say that Mr. Fletcher, but I have a lot of things to do and that was yesterday, on my schedule."

Mr. Fletcher said, "Well, Jacques, then you better re-schedule and put some order in your life. If you don't like being alive then blink five times and, I'm out of here."

"Okay, Doctor, I mean Mister:—you're right. I'll follow your instructions. Thank you for saving my life."

"You better. You have a loving wife worried to wrinkles about you and you'd better appreciate her. Don't let poison build up in you're life, man. You need to have your priorities figured out in advance."

I said, "Thank you, again. Can I see my wife and family?"

Mr. Fletcher said, "As soon as you're out of the danger zone. You're fragile lad."

"Can I have anything to drink? My mouth taste like tarmac."

Mr. Fletcher said, "I'll have me nurse give you some precious water from those good, catchy, 'Water for People' trucks. Will that do, Jacques?"

"Ouch!" I nodded and it felt like I'd had been hit by a sledgehammer.

I thought: Why is it so black in here?

When I awoke, there was a nurse tugging on my gown saying, "Your surgeon wants you to drink your water, Bwana Cuba. Can you drink this water? Now, open your mouth and don't dribble. Open wide now. Swallow. Swallow."

Can you hear me, Bwana Cuba? You have been very sick. We are here to look after you. You need to get some rest now. Go to sleep. Go to sleep."

CHAPTER NINE
CLOSE-CALL POISONS

SAFARI 37
<u>SAFARI 37</u>

Sue picked me up at Mulago. I asked her to take me to the British Embassy, as I had some urgent business. She waited for me in Reception, as I was ushered in to British Ambassador, Richard Hale's office, where I put forth my problem: re: mentioning that I have boxed, in one of my newspaper article's.

"Asinine!" Hale exclaimed. "What you did was asinine!' You have painted yourself into a corner of a small ring, my foolish friend."

I said, "I may not have been thinking straight when I sent in my article and included boxing in it. It didn't dawn on me that it would be a problem."

Hale said, "Nothing that we can't fix, my boy. Just leave it with me.

First, go back to the college and tell no one about this situation. Second, don't go to the front gate on Monday. Third, do not, at any time, communicate with anyone but me, concerning this issue. Do you understand the criteria set forth to handle this?"

I asked, "Yes. Can I tell my wife?"

"No. The less she knows the better for her."

I said, "Can I ask what your plan is?"

"I think not. All I can say is:—It will be handled, with diplomacy."

I said, "Thank you, Mr. Hale for your help with this matter."

Hale said, "It's not solely for your welfare, but that of your whole family, my friend. You don't know or appreciate what or whom you are dealing with. Good day Mr. Jacques. See you at the bridge table next Saturday, at my place."

I said, "Good day to you, Richard. See you then."

I kept my promise. When Sue asked, "What where you two talking about that was so important?—I replied, "Oh, we were just discussing some moves for the upcoming bridge game. It's at his place this Saturday. Richard and I have been paired. It's the men against the women, for the bridge matches."

Sue gave me a puzzled look, as she drove towards the College.

Mr. Hale declined to tell me what he did to defuse the situation, but from what I gathered, from keeping my ears open and mouth closed, it went something like this:

After conferring with Mr. Fletcher, he got in touch with the Ugandan High Commission where he discussed my declining physical health and how it had affected my mental health. Mr. Fletcher, Dr. Ismali and two Dr. Patel's from Rotary backed up Mr. Hale's submission.

That's as much as I could glean from my inside contacts.

We were no sooner settled at home, than the Sams appeared at our front doorstep. They had come Kampala to shop. Wally dropped

Nona and the girls, Lara and Marnie at our place and took off for downtown, to buy some samosas (an Indian delicacy).

Sue and I had a pleasant visit with Nona, while the girls and KC, under the watchful eye of Laura, played in the back yard with Lucas's son, Derrick.

When we ate lunch, but there was no sign of Wally. The day went on.

Midnight came and "not a word from Wally." We got in touch with the Police Department and alerted them of the situation. We were scared. The policeperson, we spoke to, was not at all optimistic.

At one A.M., Wally drove up, slammed on the brakes and burst into the middle of a totally worried group and shouted, "I'm alive! I'm here! I'm alive!"

He told our nervous group his story of captivity.

Wally explained, how he'd bought the samosas downtown. After getting back into his Volkswagen station wagon, he was surprised to find two African Indigenous men, brandishing pangas (machetes), in the backseat of the vehicle.

He told them, "Fellows, you must be mistaken. You're in the wrong car."

They threatened him with their blades, ordering him to drive them to Entebbe, so that they could pick up a mattress.

Wally said, "I had no choice. On the way to Entebbe, the men had twice commanded me to stop at bars. At the stops, they took the car key ring from me and went inside the bars and, after a long time, returned quite drunk."

Nona said, "Why didn't you get out and phone us?"

"We were 'off-the-beaten-track.' There were no phones and I didn't recall the Jacques's number."

Wally said, "It got dark and the two kidnappers had me stop, so they could relieve their bladders, at the side of the road. At that stop, they saw another bar and proceeded to it and luckily forgot to get the keys from me."

Wally wheeled his station wagon around and left them in the dust. After driving around for an hour or more, Wally finally found Port Bell Road and drove to a caring group of family and friends, at the Uganda College of Commerce.

Wally reported his encounter with the carjackers to the police.

The officer, who took the information, said, "Oh, such incidents are reported quite often here. You were fortunate."

The investigations of the two American missing tourists reported, "Both young men ventured up north to the Kidepo Game Park. President Amin had warned everyone not to visit this Park until a Karomojong tribe uprising had been quashed. This particular tribe had been running around in the nude or partially clad. President Amin had ordered them fully clothed or they would be shot."

Our East Indian Pipeline report stated, "Those same two Americans had tied bundles of American dollars with strings; hung these bundles inside their gas tanks and drove to Kenya, where the money had been turned over to East Indian businessmen."

This was but one method the East Indian businessman used, so he could get his money out of the country. There was an export limit of no more than 400 shillings set on East Indians, and any other foreign nationality, by the Ugandan government.

There was no information as to the recovery of the bodies of the two Americans for burial. President Amin said, "We are looking into the young men's disappearance."

Our American Pipeline informed us: "Our President contacted Amin, via, 'the red telephone,' and said, "An American ship, loaded with missiles, is stationed in the Indian Ocean, just a mile off Mombassa's shores and if one more American is missing or harmed in any way, that ship will fire directly at your Presidential residence."

In the Uganda Argus newspaper, Amin made another proclamation:—He advised all the women in Uganda not to wear mini-skirts or shorts. He was quoted as saying, "If they (the women wearing mini-skirts) continued wearing such inappropriate things they'll be jailed and the keys to the jail cell will be lost."

Back on January 1st, 1972, we had received an engraved invitation to attend the parade of tanks by President Amin and the Ugandan

Armed Forces down Kampala Road on January 25. With reserved seats in the fourth row, we sat, under our umbrellas to shield our eyes from the blazing sun, to watch the "parade of the Mighty Armed Forces." It was a long parade, over five hours long. We drank lots of iced tea from our thermoses.

All the beautiful African Palm trees, in the middle of Kampala road, had been cut down and Uganda Road had been heavily graveled and tarmaced to withstand the passage of many tanks. Most of the tanks came from the U.S.S.R. There were a few Sherman's.

Scores of Indigenous men, had so heavily occupied the rooftops of the dukas (stores), two of the rooftops collapsed and death and serious injuries had resulted.

We were sternly warned by the parade officials, "Do not to take any pictures of any sort."

Sue hid a small camera in her purse and proceeded to take pictures of President Amin in his Grand Mercury convertible, as well as the tanks and, to us, huge marching army, some 22,000 strong.

Sue said, "I need pictures for my reconnaissance evidence. We may have to show these to our Ottawa bureaucrats so they understand they are giving millions to this is an armed nation, run by a lunatic."

Meanwhile, at our home at the Uganda College of Commerce, Lucas had left Siki's (Sue's parrot) cage door unlatched and the bird had flown the coop.

I spied him way up in one of the many trees on the compound. I got my students together and they kept the parrot flying by climbing up the trees he landed on.

Finally, Siki got too tired and as he flew about a foot over my head, I jumped up and got his talons around my fingers, then fell over backwards. Sue quickly put a blanket over us, and un-griped Siki's feet from my fingers.

It was a good show of great teamwork, at its best. Sue loved that bird!

CHAPTER TEN
POISONS PILE-UP, TO PARTING

SAFARI 38

Daughter, Laura was initially enrolled at the Lincoln International American School, where many of the teachers were African-Americans. Laura was an honors student and enjoyed the schools and all its field trips to such places as:—Uganda's highest mountain, Mount Elgin. Besides American and Canadian youths, there were students from all parts of the world such as England, Sweden, Finland and Norway.

Laura started to sound like an American gal and grew to love playing baseball with the other kids and teachers, during physical education classes and recess.

Son, KC was attending a British Safari Kindergarten. All his teachers were British. He loved to learn happy things and enjoyed his friends. KC was becoming as British as Laura was becoming Americanized.

KC even said, "By Jove," just like his London-born grandpa, Charles Louis did.

We had a big scare in Uganda, the day we pulled up in front of Laura's Lincoln International School, to pick her up and take her home. In the car across the street from us, Sue spied Mabel Johnson, an American, whom we had played bridge with.

Sue went across the road and got in Mabel's big Chevrolet Biscayne car, while KC and I remained in the front seat with our dog, Bonzo on the back seat.

KC wanted to go inside the school and see Laura, so I let him out of our car on the curbside and he went into the library to get her. Bonzo and I remained in the car.

All of a sudden, I saw KC's blond head bobbing in front of our car and starting across the road and in the path of a Volkswagen Beetle car. I hit the horn and yelled as I opened the passenger door. Bonzo jumped over me and out the door running wildly. I hit the pavement with my face, rolled over and proceeded to KC.

KC had been hit into the air by the Volkswagen and was down on the pavement on the driver's side.

Before I could get to KC, two American male teachers were grabbing me and one said, "Hey, he didn't mean to hit your kid. Don't kill him!"

I answered, "I'm not going to kill anybody. I just want to get to my boy."

The School Principal kept repeating, "The driver of the car is not at fault. Your son ran right in front of his car. Don't harm the driver."

I said, "I'm not going to harm him. What's his name?"

The Principal replied, "Muhammad Ali. He's in the Ugandan Air Force and he's named after that famous American boxer. He's not at fault."

By the time I got free from the Principal and his friends, Sue had picked up KC already and was in Mabel's Biscayne Chevrolet car and the big car had whisked away to see a doctor.

Finally, Laura showed up. She'd been talking with the African-American Librarian about an interesting book.

Laura said, "Hey, dad, let's go get the dog. I think I see Bonzo over there. Then we can go to the Hospital and see how KC's doing."

Laura collected Bonzo and we quickly drove our Yellow Volkswagen to the Hospital and discovered no sign of KC or Sue or the big American car.

It was the holy holiday of "Id" and there was no medical staff on duty or call. Babies were being born in the hallways, while injured soldiers walked around with arms half cut-off. Even the receptionists were not in to work. There was bedlam and moaning.

We then returned home and Lucas said, "Memsaab Sue phoned and said, your son was being treated by a Scottish Doctor and everything was okay."

When Sue and KC arrived home, she said, "K.C. is going to be fine. It's a small world. Mabel drove us to her personal doctor, Dr. MacLean and he was in the same graduating physician's class in Edinburgh as our doctor back home, Dr. Donald.

Dr. MacLean said that the car ran over KC's foot and he had hit his head hard on the pavement. We have to keep him awake this evening and monitor how he's reacting to the pills the doctor gave us. The doctor wants to see KC on Friday. In less than a week, KC should be okay. KC is going to have a flat arch, for the rest of his life."

Even though daughter, Laura loved her experiences at the Lincoln International American School, we decided to move her to a private school in Europe because the 500 manned Uganda Army barracks, was next door. Some of the soldiers were rampaging through our College's askaris (guards) and raping any girl or woman they could find.

Sue went to a Ugandan East Indian friend, Al Leer who hurriedly and expertly arranged for us to take a trip to Europe to visit different schools for Laura. I wanted to go to Spitz, Yugoslavia to play basketball with Cal Smith, who was from there.

Al said, "Let me know your dates and leave all the details to me. Since this is only your second trip to Europe, I would suggest not going to Europe's eastern bloc. "Stay with the western world. Yugoslavia is eastern European and too much for you."

In late August of 1972, we landed in Munich. There was barbed wire as high as some buildings all around the Olympic venue. It was like a police state.

A German Police Officer, who spoke crisp English, said, "We advise you to leave Munich as soon as you can if you do not wish to go to any Olympic events."

We left Germany without looking into any schools there and proceeded to Austria and Switzerland. The Swiss schools, in Lucerne and Zurich, were three times the price of the one in Austria. The one school we looked at in Spain was not suited for a female.

After much discussion and analysis we decided on the Gloria International Girl's School in Lech, Austria. We enrolled Laura to board at Gloria's School.

At first, and for some time, Laura felt she was being sent to boarding school because we didn't love her.

We loved Laura madly and still do. She's our little princess.

I said, "Going away is for your good, Laura as there are bad men who may want to do you harm and that you'll be safer here in Lech than in Kampala. It will just be for one year and we will all be re-united at the end of that year."

Austria is quite Socialistic, in that no one person owns the land on which his or her home sits. This land the home site on belongs to the community, hence can be skied across by anyone who so desires.

Therefore, students, such as Laura, learn reading, writing and arithmetic, in the classroom, during the morning hours and ski with her classmates during the afternoon.

Lech, Austria was known for winter sports, but especially skiing.

Canada's Prime Minister, Pierre Trudeau and his wife Margaret spent a week skiing there when it was not possible for them to fly home because of the deep snowdrifts. Therefore, Prime Minister Trudeau could not attend to government business in Ottawa for that week.

When we got back to Munich, it was a "police state," because of the killing of the Israeli athletes and coaches. We were advised, "to leave immediately, if not sooner."

On the way back to Uganda, in mid-September, 1972, we stopped off at Cyprus and phoned the nearest Canadian Consulate, which was in Beirut, Lebanon. Sue had been suffering from bad stomach a pain that was not responding to any of our medicines.

I said to the young, Canadian Consulate man in Beirut, "We are four Canadians traveling back to Uganda where, through CIDA, I serve as an expatriate.

I talked to a traveler, who said there was an uprising in Uganda. I read in the British and American newspapers that Uganda is unruly and is under the siege of random killings. My wife is feeling sub-par, as she is suffering from a terrible stomachache.

Is it safe for us to go back to Uganda or should we stay in Cyprus or go back to Europe?"

The Consulate man said, "You can't believe everything you hear from a traveler and newspaper's write. We have not heard of any problems for Canadians in Uganda. You are absolutely safe to return to Uganda at your earliest convenience. It is secure. As for the wife's stomachache, I'm sure the doctors in Uganda can treat it."

I said, "Thank you. What's your name?"

He didn't answer my question. All I heard was the sound of a phone click.

We proceeded back to Uganda. As soon as we got off the plane at Entebbe, we were grabbed by two husky soldiers and relieved of our wallets and purses, where our passports were, and hustled into an interrogation room at the Entebbe airport.

A soldier, with a patch over his left eye, said, "Where have you been and for what reasons?" He proceeded to thumb through my passport while ignoring Sue's passport, where Laura and K.C. were listed.

I answered, "In Europe on vacation. My wife is not feeling well. She has to see a doctor immediately. I run three Departments at the Uganda College of Commerce and need to get back to my students immediately."

He said, "Okay, you can proceed to the Commerce but you must report to the State Bureau of Investigation office at this address, as soon as possible."

He handed me a card with an address scrawled on it.

I hailed a taxi and we went to our house at the Uganda College of Commerce, where I phoned Dr. Henry Patel and told him about Sue's sickness.

He said, "Take her to the Mulago Hospital right away. I'll meet you there in thirty minutes and will make sure that she will be attended to immediately."

True to his word, he met us at Mulago and Sue was admitted into a semi-private room, with her attending physician (surgeon) being another East Indian, Mr. Jwani.

Surgeon, Mr. Jwani said, "Has your wife had her appendix out?"

I said, "No."

Mr. Jwani said, "From where she indicates the pain is coming from, it sounds like an acute case of appendicitis. We will have to have your signed okay before we can proceed with any surgery."

I talked it over with Sue and we agreed to go ahead with the removal of her appendix.

Mr. Jwani said, "We will go ahead and prepare your wife for an appendicitis operation for tomorrow morning. It will be a short operation of no more than an hour."

The next morning, I was at the hospital early and the operation started at 8 a.m., and went on for an hour, then another hour, then another hour, then another hour and was going on another hour when I went to the medical desk and asked, "Why is my wife's operation taking so long? It was supposed to be less than an hour and now it's been four hours and still no indication that it's over."

An East Indian Intern said, "Please don't be upset, Mr. Jacques. Your wife is in good hands. Our top surgeons are doing her surgery. She is in good hands."

Another couple hours went by and then at the middle of the next hour, the Intern came over to me and said, "Your wife will be out of surgery within the hour. There were some findings that had to be explored for her betterment. Mr. Jwani will report them to you, as soon as he is available."

In 30 minutes, Mr. Jwani came to me and said, "Your wife is in good health. We took out her appendix, only to find it was perfectly healthy. Our top surgeon, Mr. Bufres found tracks of a worm in the stomach with marked surrounding inflammatory reaction. We proceeded to cut out parts of your wife's large intestine following the worm's path and found a mass of eggs the worm had laid in the intestine. To make sure we got all the worm and her eggs, we had to cut off most of the large intestine and some of the small intestine of your wife."

I asked, "Is my wife going to be in good health? What is the name of this worm?"

Mr. Jwani mumbled, "Yes, your wife will be in good health once she has sufficient rest as this was a long surgery. Here is my written appraisal of the worm."

He handed me his report and I tried to decipher his writing.

He wrote:—The tumor area thus marked eosinophilia with gnamulitin tissue tabcersses. It was most likely oesophagostime.

I asked, "Would you please put that non-medical terms Mr. Jwani?"

Mr. Jwani said, "It's been called Monkey tapeworm and most likely came from you wife eating pork. It's an anaoplaocephalid tapeworm ingested by infected mites, containing the cysteroid stage of the monkey tapeworm. I think we got all of it."

Sue was in a semi-private room for a day, and then moved to another, at my request.

In the first semi-private the other occupant of this room was Idi Amin's son, who was also a patient of Mr. Bufres. There were always two guards at the door to the room.

Idi Amin had told Mr. Bufres that if his (Amin's) son dies, then not only would Mr. Bufres die, but also all his family and his extended family and friends.

Sue spent one week in her second semi-private. The other occupant was a Bugandan woman who'd had just given birth to twin boys. Her husband and the rest of their seven children visited daily and displayed some unusual practices.

At suppertime, the father would bring a hibachi and on the hospital's window ledge cook up the family meal. After all the family, including his wife (the mother of the twins) had eaten, he would dismiss the rest of the family for them to go home and he would stay overnight in the semi-private room and would sleep under his wife's bed and sometimes on top of it, too.

Further, I had a premonition one night that all was not well with Sue at Mulago, so I got in our Yellow fastback and drove through a Kondo's (robber's) spike belt and got to my wife's room and noticed her intravenous bag was not dripping and summoned her nurse to fix it. The nurse did, but woke up Sue, when tapping on the bottle.

I asked Sue, "Are you doing well here at the hospital?"

Sue said, "I'm not getting much sleep here in this room. Perhaps, I could go home, Leo. You have to get Laura off to Austria this week."

I asked Mr. Jwani, "Is it possible for Sue to come home. She's not sleeping well in her semi-private."

Mr. Jwani said, "We would rather her stay in the hospital for at least another week, as she has lost a lot of blood and is very weak. Still, if you insist, we will release her to your care and please phone me immediately, if any complications appear."

Therefore, Sue left Mulago Hospital, for home, four days after her major operation. Lucas' wife, Maria helped out, by staying at Sue's bedside, while I was at work and Lucas was doing the shopping. Sue recovered enough in two weeks to take over the looking after of KC, shopping for food and instructing of our household staff.

When we went to Europe, we had left Sue's African Grey parrot, Siki with an Irish couple, Gordon and Myra Edwards.

After Sue was settled at home, I drove over to the Edwards to collect Siki.

Myra Edwards said, "I have good news and bad news, for you, Leo. Your Sue is alive, but her Siki is dead."

Myra had instructed her servants to look after Siki. They didn't. It seems as though Indigenous Ugandans didn't think it their place to look after the pets of musongis, unless there is a generous reward for doing it. Our friendly parrot, Siki starved to death.

In past instances, we had paid Lucas and Onyango bonuses to look after our dog, Bonzo, as well as Siki.

This time we had paid them to look after the dog only and thought Myra would care for the bird. She had said, "Looking after a bird is as easy as getting a tennis ace."

Sue forgave Myrna's servants for starving her beloved Siki, and still gave her the present she'd bought her in Europe.

Sue said, "After all, he was only a parrot. Humans die, in this country, daily."

I had to get an okay from the Uganda Government, in order to buy a ticket, to fly Laura out to Europe. This requirement had just been put in place, shortly before we arrived back at Entebbe.

I spent the better half of a day, waiting in long lines to get the approval for Laura's flight to Austria. The government man, who handled my request, was or the Nubian tribe that served as bodyguards for President Amin. The man labored at the task of approving forms. It seemed to take forever, but it, in reality was only eight hours.

In order to get money for Laura in Austria, Sue shoved it into "modesss" pads.

The guards at the airport went through Laura's luggage like a fine toothcomb, but didn't handle the "modess" pads.

It was a tearful goodbye at the Entebbe Airport, as we had come to Uganda as a family of four and now we were three. Still, it was the right thing to do for Laura's safety. At the time, there was so much uncertainty in Uganda. Amin's army was raiding stores and houses looking for anything they desired. In general, they created chaos all over the country.

SAFARI 39

Jinja-town is the second biggest municipality in Uganda. All of the country's hydroelectric power comes from Jinja's big, Owen Falls Dam. The Dam enticed many industries to the town, as well as luring many Indigenous African workers.

Jinja-town claims to be the source of the Nile river and here you can discuss electric power over what the local people love:—Nile beer and crumpets.

Jinja-town is a popular destination for backpackers going white-water rafting. Canoeing, Kayaking and Body Surfing are also popular.

This urbanization movement attracted many dukas and market places, as well as many church denominations. The dukas were one hundred percent owned by Ugandan East Indians. The market places, are where the Indigenous Africans, sold their wares. The Roman Catholic Church was the dominant religion in Jinja.

The Principal of the Uganda College of Commerce, M.C. Abliba came to me and said, "I want you to take your very best students to

Jinja to visit the Manavani Sugar Factory as well as the dukas, markets and the large dam."

I said, "Could I ask why you are making this request?"

She said, "Our esteemed President has requested it of you?"

I said, "Why didn't he come ask me."

She said, "He is much to busy to see you right now. What is your decision?"

I answered, "I will work it into my weekly schedule, Ms. Abliba."

The top ten students of my Department of Distribution (Marketing) & Business were selected to accompany me to Jinja-town via our departmental Safari van.

The students selected were:—nine young men and one young lady. The young lady, Mrs. Angela Buka led the class, in marks. She was a Bugandan, who had taken a leave of absence from her drugstore (Poison store), in order to take our six-month course. Her husband,

David ran their business, while she was in the course. Angela called the drugs in their store, "poisons."

Her classmates knew Angela as:—"The Poison Lady."

Before leaving the Uganda College of Commerce, I went to Principal, Ms. Abliba to confirm the trip, but could not locate her on campus or elsewhere.

I thought: This is strange. She's usually easy to contact.

Nevertheless, the trip was, "a go," and we hit the road for Jinja-town.

When we got to the Manavani Sugar Factory at noon, armed soldiers greeted us at the gates. They looked menacing at our Bugandan van driver, Roy Bamino and said, "State your business here? This is the residence of our esteemed leader."

I answered, "We are from the Uganda College of Commerce and have a pre-arranged tour of the Sugar Factory by President Amin and our Principal, Ms. Abliba."

The Head Guard said, "Do you have any documentation authorizing this tour?"

I said, "No, but you can phone either our College at this number or ask the President's clerk and either will verify our visit."

After an hour delay in the hot sun, we were instructed to proceed through the gates. During that hour, I exchanged my sandwiches with four students who were curious as to what I ate for lunch. Their food comprised of matoke and rice, soaked in the oils from different trees. It was plain and palatable.

Our Bugandan driver, Roy Bamino said to me, "I will drop you off here as I have to get a fan belt for the van in town. It will require at least 15 shillings. I will come back to these gates for you in five hours. Is that fine with you, Bwana Cuba?"

I said, "Okay. We will be expecting you then. Here is 20 shillings for the belt."

We proceeded to the residence by foot and were greeted by President Amin.

He said, "Welcome to my sugar factory. You will not be able to go through it today as my men are working very hard for the good of our country."

Before I could answer, a soldier jabbed a gun in my ribs and escorted us back to the front gate.

I did ask, "What has become of, Mr. Matovani, the previous factory owner?"

"Oh, he sold it and moved to Kenya. He no longer owns this factory."

I asked, "How far are we from Jinja town?"

The Head Guard said, "It is but a short distance from here. You can walk it easily."

There was a steep hill to climb on our path to town. Along the path was the decaying corpse of a young lady. Her arms had been wired behind her back and both her hands had been cut off, at the wrist.

I asked Angela, "What has happened here?"

Angela said, "It appears this young woman was a thief. That is why her hands have been cut off. From the decay of her body, I believe she was killed by a panga at least two or three days ago."

From this vantage point, I could see a church and I said, "There are three nuns entering that church down there. Let's go down and I will ask them if they can help."

When we got to the church, I asked the group of three nuns, "Are you aware that there is a body of a young Indigenous woman on the trail of the hill up there?"

One Sister answered, "Oh yes, we are aware of her body."

I said, "What happened? Why is her body left up there to rot?"

Sister said, "She was caught stealing and the soldiers killed her, cut off her hands and threw her body from the top of the hill, to serve as a deterrent for such a crime. She was left to rot because she was not a member of our Church."

I said, "What will it take to have your Church give her a proper burial?"

Sister said, "One hundred shillings."

I handed her the money and said, "Please attend to her as soon as possible because she is decomposing."

We went into town and visited five dukas and two market places to observe the owner's and laborers at work. I questioned my students as to what business practices they had seen and whether they could be improved on or not?"

We went to the Shell Station in town, to enquire as to the whereabouts of our driver. Both workers at the Shell were fast asleep.

Finally, we found our driver, Roy in a downtown bar, sipping Waragi (local whiskey).

Roy said, "I have bought the fan belt. It was 15 shillings, so I am drinking five shillings worth of Waragi."

Everybody got back in our van and our tipsy Roy drove towards Owens Dam.

Suddenly, there was a loud cracking sound and our van jarred to a halt. The new fan belt spewed on the road. I asked the Roy, "To check as to what was wrong?

Roy answered, "I am hired to be a driver and that's all I do. I am no mechanic."

After getting the bonnet (hood) open on the van, I saw only shreds of rubber where the fan belt had bust. I thought:—This new fan belt is history!

Since we were stopped on the side of a hill and the van was slowing going backwards, I asked all the students to get out and help push the van up the incline. They gladly got behind the van and preceded to chat and display a different character than the one I had witnessed to date.

The young men kept pinching Angela in the rear and trying to wrestle her into the ditch. They showed no respect for the fact that she was a married woman.

I intervened and Angela turned on me and with hatred in her flashing eyes, and said, "What they are doing is okay with me. Do not interfere, Bwana Cuba!"

I was dumbfounded and unaware of this change in behavior of, not only the boys, but of Angela as well. We were no longer in a classroom, for sure.

I said, "Look, if you want to fool around, do it on your own time, not mine. It's five o'clock and darkness is falling, so let's get this van up the hill so we can go home."

With that, the group pushed the van, with the driver in it, up the hill. While we were pushing up the hill, I spied three women washing their dishes in the stream that ran along the side of the road.

When we got stopped, I asked Roy, the driver, "Did you keep the old fan belt?"

Roy said, "Yes, but it is near broken."

I said, "Give it to me. Do you have something I can will carry water in."?

Roy repeated, "I am a driver only. I am not a pitcher provider."

I took the old fan belt and went to the group of woman washing their dishes and said, "May I buy a big jar to hold water in it for our van?"

A lady answered, "Yes, we have a jar that will hold water. You pay us 20 shillings for it, yes?"

I paid the lady her asking price and filled up the jar with water that I poured into the radiator. Subsequently, I put the old fan belt back on the van. Since, water was leaking from the radiator, I took a piece of cloth off my raincoat, Sue had insisted I take, and jammed it in the hole.

I had Roy turn the van towards Kampala and back to the College.

It was dusk and the branches from the big trees on both sides of the road were thatched together and only tiny streams of light got through.

Africa is "the Darkest-Continent," after five o'clock. No lights or yellow lines on the highway. When pitch-black, many animals, especially large cats, are on the move.

With nothing to guide our tipsy driver, our van slowly crawled home. We arrived back at the College at 9:30 p.m. It took us four hours to go a little over 60 miles.

Along the way, I led the group in a singsong and kept my eye on what Angela was doing. I had to shake her arm several times to get her out of the embrace of a male.

She was very promiscuous and I had to continually inform her, "You are a married woman. Act like one."

Angela sassed back, "Not tonight. Tonight is my uhuru (independence) day."

When we arrived home, Sue said, "I thought you'd never get back. I was worried. Why so late?"

I explained roughly what had happened and asked Sue, "Have you seen Ms. Baliba today?"

Sue said, "No. I haven't seen hide or hair of her."

The next morning, I inquired at the College, "As to wither Ms. Baliba was?"

The Bursar, who answered under the cloak of anonymity, said, "She's been taken away by members of the Secret Police:—The State Research Bureau."

I asked, "Do you know why?"

He said, "Rumor has it, she's been accused of disgraceful behavior in office."

I phoned the Department of Education office and asked, "I want to speak to someone concerning the whereabouts of my Principal at the Uganda College of Commerce?"

I was told by the clerk, "Please, for your own good, do not press us for this."

Two days later, the Bursar interrupted my morning business class.

He said, "Amin is in your new College office and wants to speak to you immediately."

I quickly assigned my students a business case for them to work on and solve and went to the new College building and met with Amin, dressed in his Presidential garb, with lots of shining medals dangling. Two burly, bodyguards accompanied him.

Amin said, "Next week, I want you to represent Uganda at The Institute of Management Conference in Munich, Germany and when you come back, to become the new Principal of this College."

I answered, "Is not Ms. Baliba the Principal?"

He said, "No. She has been removed from office. That is why I am asking you to take over right away."

I said, "I am appreciative of your offers, but I most graciously decline as I . . ."

Interrupting, Amin said, "I am offering you a nice trip and a big promotion. You can ask your government to contribute towards your Management trip to Germany. I am sure they will approve it. Your office here will be five times the size of this one we are in right now. You let me know your approval at, 'The Big Tent Celebration' of the College's new buildings this coming Saturday."

With that, he clicked his heels together, pivoted, stomped out, got in his limousine and was whisked away, in a cloud of red dust.

I thought: Our time here is numbered. Time for more planning; quicker action.

When I got home, I explained to Sue what had happened and that we were expected to be at "The Big Tent," this coming Saturday.

Sue said, "We better go to the celebration. If he talks to you, you tell him that you'll have to talk this over with Ottawa, before you can make any decisions, Leo."

That Saturday afternoon, we went to a Christening of the daughter our Irish friends, Gordon and Myra Edwards.

They were calling her Avis. Avis stood for "star," in their Irish language.

Myra Edwards was also an Accounting teacher in Professional Studies. All her students were at the well-attended Christening. There were over 100 people present.

Myra went about telling everyone in hearing distance, "Just ten years ago, when I was 18, and meant to marry this older Irish gentleman from a prosperous Dublin family, I eloped with my Private Club's tennis pro, Gordon and we left on a plane to Uganda, never to return to Ireland."

She added, "When I got a post teaching Accounting at the College, many of the students thought I was also a student, rather than a teacher, because I looked so young."

Gordon piped in, "They don't make that mistake now, do they Myra."

We all laughed at their light humor.

As well as their leader, Mr. Leeky, many of the College's Instructors from Professional Studies were in attendance.

That sunny afternoon, many of the Indigenous students, "hung one on."

Gordon had rented one of the few donkeys in Uganda for the occasion.

We muzongis (whites) took turns riding a donkey.

Myra said, "It was like a bunch of Asses riding an ass."

I answered, "Yes. All had a good time playing cowboy."

On Saturday evening, Sue dressed in a lovely sari. She looked beautiful.

I wore my best safari suit.

We walked over to the "Big Tent," where the celebration of the opening of the new College buildings, was held.

There was a long dark tunnel leading into the big tent and we went in arm-in-arm. Along the way, Sue kept jumping around and bumping into to me.

Sue stopped and said, "Leo, turn around and go back quickly and out the entrance."

We did a pivot and got out pronto. I asked, "Why did you want to leave? Are you not feeling well?"

Sue said, "I was being mauled and pinched in there. I can't go back."

"Okay, let's go home."

So, we went back home and didn't attend the celebration, in the "Big Tent."

I thought: Those who pinched Sue must be cat people. They do their prowling and are aggressive when the darkness is pitch black like ebony.

The next morning, we received six parrots (three yearlings and three babies) from a Devon Smith, a Canadian stationed in Nakuru, Kenya. The parrots had been bought by another Canadian, Sean Bond who had left Kampala with his wife, Mitzi and their three "K" boys: Keith, Kerry and Kent.

Bond had bought the parrots from Joe Matoke, an Indigenous African for six dollars a piece.

He had asked Devon Smith to bring them to us so that we could ship them, or have someone else, ship them to Canada.

We quickly got in touch with the Canadian Officials to make arrangements for the birds to be shipped to Canada. The parrots were on their way by the next day.

They arrived in Bolton airport in Toronto.

Each of the three babies died en-flight.

The survivors were sent to Ottawa. Two of the three surviving yearlings lived after that inspection.

On arrival, in Hamilton, Bond sold one to a pet store and kept the other, he called, Jo.

Bond kept Jo for 31 years, during which time; he conversed with the smart bird, every morning.

Subsequently, Bond offered Jo to Sue because he knew that she loved African Grey Parrots and had lost both of hers:—Siki in Kampala and the one I had bought for her that was called, Punch, in Red Deer County.

Sue turned Bond's kind and generous offer down.

Bond then sold Jo to a know-it-all collector in Toronto for $600.

SAFARI 40

Fear spread quickly through the entire East Indian and expatriate community. There was a daily East Indian Message Advisory Report concerning what days or times of day was safe, or not safe, to leave home for work or shopping in Kampala.

One hundred Libyan troops had been sent by the Libyan leader, Colonel Muammar Gaddafi, to Uganda. Ugandan troops had mistaken them for East Indians and had shot 50 of them. The Libyan's bodies were just left to rot in the streets.

My East Indian Rotary members told me the latest story going on via the East Indian grapevine. It was about the Libyans and Amin's stooges.

I will relate this top East Indian Rotary story to you, as it goes as follows:—

Amin got his wings (flying airplanes safely) in Israel, but since he had expelled the Jews from Uganda and Gaddafi had adopted him as a son-in-law, the Ugandan despot had sent 100 of his favored tribe to

Libya to be trained as pilots. In turn, Gaddafi sent 100 of his troops to Uganda to look after his son-in-law.

When Gaddafi heard Amin's goons mistook the Libyans to be East Indians and had killed 50 of his (Gaddafi's) men, he in turn had 50 of the Ugandan leader's pilot trainees, in Tripoli, shot.

Irate, Amin got in the jet he had loaned from the Libyan leader and flew to Tripoli to voice his disapproval of the killing of his pilot trainees.

When Amin met with Gaddafi, the latter said, "I have a riddle for you, Idi," while brushing aside what the Ugandan leader was there for.

Amin stopped in his tracks and listened.

Gaddafi said, "Who is my father's son, but not my brother?"

Amin thought and thought and thought and finally said, "I don't know."

Gaddafi said, "Myself."

Amin forgot all about his deceased pilot trainees, hurriedly jetted back to Entebbe and called his War Council together, in Kampala, and addressed them with:—"I have a riddle for you from Colonel Gaddafi. It is:—Who is my father's son but not my brother?"

The members of the War Council debated this riddle for hours, but couldn't come up with an answer.

The spokesperson for the War Council said, "We don't know. Who is it?"

With a pompous smile on his face, Amin answered, "Colonel Gaddafi."

When telling this story, the East Indian laughed so hard, tears ran down his cheeks and he said, "Out of all our misery, we love humor."

It was time to get our Canadian representative group mobile, to discuss the effects of such edicts and actions and their effect on the Canadians serving in Uganda.

Disguised as a Christmas Party, the first meeting had been held at the Grand Hotel, back on December 23, 1971, just before we pushed off on our Pygmy Safari.

Sue was elected to head the "Concerned Canadian Group" or, as it was known, "the C.C.G.," with weekly meetings of the executive and semi-monthly meetings of the remaining, interested body.

From the middle of January till mid-October, 1972, couples visited our place for supper with discussions about:—"How things are proceeding with 'the C.C.G.?"'

Through our East Indian friends, we had inside sources and kept everyone informed as to what had been "going down" lately.

We became good friends with John and Joan Grant of St. Paul, Minnesota.

John and I had a great time playing Athenian soldiers, for the play, "The Lysistrata of Aristophanes," put on by Uganda's National Theatre April 27 to 29, 1972?

I will always remember, how the gals playing the Greek women decided that war had been a man's affair long enough. They took it onto themselves to dislodge us Athenian soldiers by throwing us off the stage, hoping that act would bring lasting peace.

Most of the women in that play were British secretaries, who had worked 18 months straight. They deferred time off until the end of these 18 months and looked forward to taking four-month vacation.

The British underground told us the following story:—One of the British ladies, Peggy Lane was subject to a roadblock by the Ugandan army. A soldier asked her for her passport and when she was too slow giving it to him, the soldier had viscously used his rifle butt to smash in the side of Peggy's once-pretty face.

Peggy was the daughter of a high-ranking British educator and he had his Embassy, arrange to put her on the first-available British plane to London, so she could be operated on, as soon as possible.

The happening upset the whole British establishment in Uganda.

It was one terrible incident of many.

From the East Indian grapevine, we heard the following story: Two turban-headed Sikh men were shot to death, by two Ugandan soldiers, during a scuffle over gold bracelets and necklaces, that had been hidden in the Sikh lady's clothing.

The soldiers had stopped the two Sikh families from leaving Uganda by bus and started unraveling the lady Sikhs robes. The two husbands took exception to this and fought the soldiers.

It was the Sikhs men's bare hands against the loaded guns of the soldiers and the guns prevailed and both Sikh men died a warrior's death.

The rumor mill was rampart with similar shocking stories.

Our hearts went out to the families of the people involved. We prayed for those who were left:—For their healing and survival.

The front page of the Uganda Argus:—The Voice of Africa, was as follows:

"ALL ASIANS MUST GO—President's new phase in the 'economic war'—PRESIDENT Idi Amin said at the weekend that

all the 23,000 Asians who hold Uganda citizenship will also have to leave the country, in addition to the 60,000 who have already been ordered to quit."

I was shocked, at the two-page ad from two English cities, which ran in the Uganda Argus in:

THESE ADS WERE LARGE, DARK, <u>UNDERLINED NOTICES AS FOLLOWS</u>:

<u>**AN IMPORTANT ANNOUNCEMENT ON BEHALF OF THE CITY OF _____, ENGLAND**</u>

The City Council of _____, England believes that many families in Uganda are considering moving to _____.

If YOU are thinking of doing so, it is very important you should know that PRESENT CONDITIONS IN THE CITY ARE VERY DIFFERENT FROM THOSE MET BY EARLIER SETTLERS.

They are:

HOUSING—several thousands of families are already on the Council's waiting list

EDUCATION—hundreds of children are awaiting places in the schools

SOCIAL AND HEALTH SERVICES—already stretched to the limit

IN YOUR OWN INTERESTS AND THOSE OF YOUR FAMILY YOU SHOULD ACCEPT THE ADVICE OF THE UGANDA RESETTLEMENT BOARD AND NOT COME TO _____.

These ads ran for week after week, near the front of the daily newspaper, the Uganda Argus, The Voice of Africa.

On the next page to the English city's ads were the following:

CANADA

CANADIAN HIGH COMMISSION IMMIGRATION SERVICE INTERVIEWS

I.P.S. BUILDING, KAMPALA

Holders of the following reference numbers are invited to appear for interview **MONDAY, 25, SEPT. 72, 8:30 TO 11.00 AND 2.00 TO 4.00.**

There were hundreds and hundreds of numbers under these timetables.

Below them was:

Medical examination will take place the same day; married persons with dependants (wife, children) must bring their dependants with them if they reside in Uganda.

Only those persons whose REFERENCE NUMBERS appear above will be interviewed. All OTHER holders of reference numbers should refrain from contacting this office unless invited to do so.

On the next page, there was a cartoon of a plump musongu (white person) lying on a carpet next to a bed, with a HOME SWEET HOME sign hanging on the wall, as he perks up his ear and listens to his Mama muzazi (mother) as she says, "O.K. SO I'VE PRESSED YOUR TROUSERS, IRONED YOUR SHIRT, POLISHED YOUR BOTTLE OPENER. NOW GET UP OFF THE FLOOR WHERE YOU'VE SLEPT ALL NIGHT—JUMP ON YOUR BIKE, AND

GO AND SHOW ME WHAT A CLEVER LITTLE SHOP KEEPER YOU ARE."

The caption below the cartoon was: Now is the time for Ugandans to roll their sleeves up and get down to work and prove they can run the economy of the country. Opportunity is knocking.

The streets and avenues of Kampala told a grime story of rampart crime.

The guard gates at many East Indian homes were wide open and their places were looted by unruly mobs, lead by the Ugandan Army men and their friends.

It was impossible to get a taxi ride, as most of the East Indian cabs had all doors open and hoods up. The bars at the dukas (stores) had been pried open and all the merchandise, including clothes and food, flung around, with a lot of it on the red earth. Buses and bicycles were all over the place and the food markets were under siege.

I received a phone call from a quiet spoken Army Intelligence Officer, asking me to report, at 8 am, on this date, to the State Bureau of Research, at the same address the Army Officers, at the Entebbe airport, had given me in September, after we had come back home from Europe.

The address was a downtown building, and when I said I had an appointment with the State Bureau of Research, I was told to stand in a lineup to get into the office.

After an hour's wait, I got into the office. It was bare, except for one steel-folding chair. Two Army Officers came in, swinging small repeat-shooters that looked like small, "Tommie-guns," around my head. I flipped down dark shades over my glasses and sat down and looked them in the eye. I felt the breeze from the twirling and thought: Act cool. Don't rush. Don't show fear. One's eyes are the windows to the soul.

The elder Officer of the two said, "What is your business here?"

I said, "Yesterday, I was telephoned by Army Intelligence to come here."

The elder said, "Show me your passport. Always have it ready for us to see."

I nodded and put my passport in his hand.

He said, "We heard that you are shipping your automobile to Nairobi. Why are you doing this, and concerning your daughter, will she be coming back to Uganda shortly?"

I said, "I've decided to move my car to Nairobi so that I can use it there when I go for a Kenyan vacation. My daughter will be spending this school term in Europe."

He nodded his head to the other who dug his gun into my ribs a few times.

The elder said, "You are not answering my questions. How are you going to get to Kenya without your car and will she be coming back to Uganda shortly?"

I said, "Oh, I plan to fly on Uganda Airways to Nairobi and my daughter is in school in Europe and will be there for the school term."

He nodded again.

The other Officer left the room and returned with a tea caddy.

The elders said, "Do you want some tea?"

I answered, "Yes. That would be nice. Thank you."

Then the younger Officer rammed the tea caddy into my legs, drew it back and thrust it heavily against my legs again. I kept silent, then sprung to my feet.

I sternly said, "WHY ARE YOU DOING THESE ACTS TO ME, OFFICER? EXPLAIN YOURSELF MISTER!"

With a stunned look on his face, the younger Officer stepped back and nearly fell backwards. I sat down and the elder Officer moved so close to me I could smell his whiskey-breathe.

He said, "We are testing you to find truth. It is up to us to find out truth. We will let you go home for now. You come back tomorrow and line-up at 8 am, to see us then."

His lips broke into an ever-widening smile and he flipped my passport in my lap.

With that, they both clicked their heels together and went out of the room. I got up and staggered out the door and into the hallway.

When I got out on the street, I saw my Goan friend, John Mack. He suggested we go to a coffee shop and have a chat.

He said, "Don't talk to me about what you just experienced, until we get to this safe haven."

I thought:—No way was I coming back to that place, tomorrow.

I said, "I think I made a mistake going there in the first place. I sure have sore ribs and shins."

John said, "I don't think you realized, who the people were, that you saw today. Those two, were interrogating members of the State Bureau of Research. That's a fancy name for the poisonous hench-men who are Amin's Gestapo. The State Bureau men do a lot of his killings. If you go back, you most likely would be taken to Makindye Prison and you'd be tortured and possibly exterminated. Leave Uganda, my friend. Go back to Canada, or better yet, come to Australia with me and my family."

I said, "You're right about the State Bureau. I won't make the same mistake twice. Hey, you didn't tell me you were moving to Australia. We had hoped you and your lovely wife, Mary and family would come to Canada."

John said, "Alas, we have all lived in relatively hot weather all our life. We originally came from Goa, before it was taken over by India. It's warmer than Uganda. We're destined to move to Sydney, Australia. Please give me your home address in Canada and once we're all settled, we can correspond, my friend. Sue and you have always been warm with us."

When I got home and told Sue what went down. She said, "Why didn't you check with me first? I could have found out just what those people are and what this State Research Bureau was really all about. You have to trust me to find these things out for you, Leo."

I said, "Surely you don't think I should go back there tomorrow?"

She said, "No way. You will see only Canadians or friends of Canadians next time, Leo. You're not going to go to any more places like that one? Right?"

"Right as rain."

I thought: What I considered my small successes here will be of no consequence. I will not be remembered not so much for what I learned, but for what I taught. I like to be recalled, not for any act of courage, but for my having compassion for other humans.

Even though I tried to help out people who are under the auspices of Amin, that man is a tyrant, first thought to be nothing more than a buffoon.

It seems like any bridges built have or are in the process of being dynamited.

Still, I pray that we, as a family, tried our best to aid others less fortunate than ourselves and that these others will survive this poisonous Despot and thrive in the future.

CHAPTER ELEVEN
CUT-ADRIFT BY
CLOAK-AND-DAGGER

SAFARI 41

Back on July 4th, 1972, Sue and I had enjoyed a wonderful time with John and Joan Grant when we enjoyed an America's Independence Day with a delicious barbeque of New York steaks on Spider Island, out in Lake Victoria.

It was the Grant's way of thanking us for having them over for super at our place in the Uganda College of Commerce.

John worked for the American Embassy and had his own Spitfire airplane, he'd purchased from the Israelis for nine thousand dollars. He used this plane to make money from anyone interested in seeing Uganda from the air.

John had said to me, "I'll take you for a flight up to that Kidepo Game Park when it's safe, Leo. There are different types of animals in that arid region of this country that you'll love. For a equine lover like you, you'll see Zebras."

"I look forward to that trip, John. Too bad your plane's only a two-seater. Sue would love to see the Zebras, too."

John told us how he'd been initiated into their 'Embassy Group' by a dirty trick. He and Joan were devout Christians.

The leaving of a naked indigenous girl (a jungle bunny), in a basket, on their house's front doorstep had caused unnecessary friction between his Joan and him. It took John over a week of explaining. He said, "I knew nothing about this set-up."

John had distanced himself from those he considered responsible for the prank.

Nevertheless, John was determined to perform his Embassy duties.

He was well informed about what the American government was doing to ensure the safety of its citizens in Uganda.

The Americans were on Step two of their five-point plan, and, we were informed, the British were on the seventh step of their ten-point plan. Canada had no plan, yet.

We lost touch with John and Joan around the middle of October in 1972. They didn't answer phone calls and they had left their Kampala house in haste.

The American Embassy was hush-hush on them or their whereabouts.

Our East Indian pipeline informed us: "John's plane had been taken from him by Amin's goons and the American Embassy had got it back for him. When John, with Joan, was back flying the plane, it was shot down by Ugandan artillery fire. It appears that neither John nor Joan Grant survived the crash."

Sue and I were sad when we heard the fate of our friends and hoped the report was mistaken and that they were safe and well.

Our Concerned Canadian Group's escape plan was 'in the works.' The nearest Canadian Embassy was in Nairobi, Kenya. Sue forwarded a report to that Embassy with pictures she had taken of the Ugandan army and all their weaponry and tanks.

Sue had no such visions of Amin being anything but a man of poison.

She kept telling me: "We should consider getting both kids to a safe haven."

"Laura's already safe in a boarding school in Lech, Austria. Where's such a place for K.C.? He's only four and too young to be separated from you."

It was a problem we were constantly aware of:—What to do with K.C. and Sue in case of all out war? Who could we turn to and how could we get out of Uganda safely?

Both our Canadian Government Ugandan Liaisons had been non-existent and non-communicative.

The East Indian Pipeline told us:—"We have heard that the Uganda Argus editor, Tom Williams had resigned and now lives in Rhodesia with his family."

Another edition of this never-ending rumor mill was: "Ex-C.I.D.A. Liaison, Tom Wood was living in Switzerland with his family."

They also reported:—"Harold Baker lost his Baker's Cabins in Mombassa to the Kenyan government, by expropriation and he had quit his position in England and retuned to Kenya and was now working as the Cabin's manager for Jomo Kenyatta's country."

In late October, 1972, Catrina Porter made a one-day appearance at the Uganda International Hotel and summoned Sue and me to come up and meet with her. She would not leave the safety of this guarded hotel. She said Canada was withdrawing her expatriates shortly. She trembled the whole time she was in our presence, in fear.

Sue had asked Porter, "What should we be telling the Canadians here?'

Porter said, "A Canadian man will be bringing a cavalcade of cars from Nairobi into Kampala to meet with you and all other Canadians, but you must understand C.I.D.A.'s main thrust right now is to interview, select and move the East Indians from Uganda to Canada as they are the ones who are being attacked and are not safe here."

Sue said, "How ready should Canadian Expatriates be for evacuation from here?" Porter said, "Remember, you will have to wait your turn to be airlifted out. Just make sure that you inform the rest of the Canadians here to pack up and be ready to leave at a moment's notice."

She added, "When the Canadian cavalcade comes in from Kenya, there will be a Douglas Roberts, who serves in the Canadian Embassy in Nairobi and he will be available to meet with all Canadians serving in Uganda to help with visas as well as transport or disposal of automobiles and other big items.

We called a meeting of all Canadian Expatriates in Uganda to meet at a Kampala school hall we rented on November 2, 1972.

Sue informed all those that attended as to what Catrina Porter had said to us and made a point to emphasize the "leaving at a moment's notice" part.

Sue also told those who were in attendance:—"All you Canadians who are here have to inform those not here of to what has gone on here. If you know of someone that you can't get in touch with, please let us know immediately and we will personally tell them what is happening. Please let me or Leo know the names of those people we have to contact."

After the meeting, I went over to the Kampala International Hotel and checked with the front desk clerk to find out whether a Douglas Roberts from Nairobi had checked or was due to check in.

The clerk was, Ram Bayoun an ex-student of mine at U.C.C., and I asked him to keep my query in: "the strictest confidence."

Ram said, "My lips are sealed Bwana Cuba. I will phone you immediately when Mr. Roberts arrives."

Three days later, the Canadian Cavalcade of cars and jeeps came down Kampala Road with much adieu. Uganda's East Indian citizens cheered them even louder than the Expatriate Canadians.

As our East Indian Rotarian friend, Dr. Henry Patel said, "Your country is offering us life. Soon, in Uganda, there will be no sun, no moon and no days to live for us. Your country has opened its arms to us. Many British cities have taken out big ads in the Uganda Argus daily newspaper telling us not to come to their city, as we will not be welcomed. These British places tell us, to stay away from them."

He added, "Canada is opening up its arms to all of us.

Australia, with their gigantic bottle of Scotch Whiskey as their emblem, will take no more than a dozen of us and only if our skin is a very light hue."

He went on, "The United States has been silent on accepting any of us, as has New Zealand, Germany, France, Belgium and any other European or Asian Country.

Many of us have dual citizenship with Ugandan and British passports and we expected Great Britain to welcome us in like Canada has."

I said, "Yes, I saw the British ads in the Argus and the weeklies. I pray that Great Britain will grant its own passport holders asylum."

The Uganda Argus continued to run the heading: "ASIANS MILKED THE COW: THEY DID NOT FEED IT—GEN. AMIN. PRESIDENT Amin has disclosed that he would summon the British High Commission to make arrangements and remove the 80,000 Asian British passport holders within three months."

Ram Bayou phoned and informed me that a Doug Roberts had checked in.

Sue phoned Mr. Roberts and told him who she was and that she was interested in meeting with him concerning my family's safety and: "How he could expedite our car out of Uganda and to a place where it could be sold."

Mr. Roberts said, "Just call me Doug, Sue. You don't have to be formal. We're Canadians aren't we. Let me look at my schedule right now and I'll meet with you as soon as possible. I'm from British Columbia and we have ways of moving things."

Sue said, "Okay, Doug. Can I make the appointment now or will you phone me?"

Doug said, "I've just looked at my calendar and I have an opening at 8 tomorrow morning. Would you be so kind as to come to the International then?"

Sue said, "Okay, but I want my husband, Leo to meet with you as I can't make it as I have to look after my very young son."

Doug said, "Fine and dandy. I forgot to tell you to have Leo bring all the information as to ownership of your car and your air and sea shipment lists with him."

The first question Doug asked me was, "Did you bring all the documentation?"

I said, "Yes, here it is. Everything is in this bundle."

Doug said, "I've filled out these forms with as much as I can and need you to insert your car's info on the open spaces. We'll get it away to Nairobi later today if all things go well. Now, I have these B.C. Government official stamps to put to good use on your documents. The more I stamp the better. At least that's what I have found in dealing with the people at the border. They just love having everything stamped."

I filled out all the pertinent information about our car. It had been a solid buy and had withstood the wild Cape Buffaloes. After that fiasco, I had taken it to a shop repairman to have all the dents pounded out and the Volkswagen fastback repainted. It looked appealing to go along with a great motor.

Doug stamped and stamped and stamped and signed and signed and signed, then smiling said, "Leo. Leave me your car and I'll do my best to put it on the Kampala to Nairobi run tonight. It'll be shipped in a boxcar and will have the proper ID forms for us to pick it up shortly after it arrives. We'll pick up your sea shipment today and have it in Mombassa by the day after tomorrow. Either Catrina Porter or I will be in touch with you as soon as we possibly can. Is that okay with you?"

I said, "Yes, Doug. Here is the extra set of keys. Everything about the car is on your desk and the owner's manual is in the passenger side glove box. Is that okay?"

"Sure thing, Leo. It was a pleasure to meet you and assist you in any way I can. Of course, Catrina informed you that Canada's main thrust right now is to offer the East Indian population in Uganda safe voyage to our great country. These East Indians will be great citizens and we will take all that are willing to come. Pierre has spoken!"

We shook hands and that was the last time we saw each other.

Doug was a credit to our Country and was performing an important job for Canada.

SAFARI 42

At my Uganda College of Commerce office, I had another unexpected visit from Idi Amin, dressed in his khaki army fatigues.

He said, "You here for the good of Uganda?"

I answered, "Yes, I am here for the good of the people of Uganda. How can I help you today, Mr. President?" I wondered if he recalled my missing the "Big Tent" celebration and not giving him an answer to his offer?

He said, "You must become the next Principal of this College and put more research and teachings for the future Ugandan Indigenous duka owners. I have had a message from God and he has told me to expel all the Asians from Uganda. The Asians have only milked the cow, but did not feed it to yield more milk."

I thought: He must have forgotten about his already offering me the Principal-ship and to represent the Uganda Institute of Management in Germany.

I said, "I feel honored that you offer me the Principal's post at the Uganda College of Commerce, but I am happy with what I am presently doing here."

He said, "You are not aware that I have ordered the construction of a new Trader's building here on these grounds. Your Principal office will be fifty times as big as this one and your lecture rooms will hold over 400 students and be very, very modern. How can you refuse such a generous offer? I demand your answer no later than noon tomorrow."

With that, he clicked his heels together, spun around and departed.

I went home, talked it over with Sue, and then phoned Mr. Hale at the British Consulate.

After explaining to Hale what Amin had said, the British High Commissionaire said, "I think it is time for you to leave, old boy. I'll have two of my men over at your place first thing tomorrow morning. Do not try to communicate or visit with me and don't repeat my name over the phone again. Pack lightly. Get ready to move quickly."

The next day was havoc in Kampala. Sirens and loud noises permeated the air.

Two Brits showed up at our house at 6 a.m., and after showing me their Secret Service I.D's, the one identified as Mr. Brown said, "Your wife and son will come with us to go to the Lake Victoria Hotel in Entebbe for a week before you join them and fly out."

I asked, "What am I going to be doing for that week?"

Brown said, "We will return for you and give you further instructions of how you wind up your affairs here."

When they came back for me, I asked, "How are my wife and family? What's their room number?"

After receiving the room number from them, I phoned and said, "Sue, do you have any feelings of doubt in what's going on?"

Sue said, "No. I feel that we are in good hands. No use talking on phone. It might be bugged. 'Bye, honey."

The Brits took me to a house just off Kampala Road.

Brown said, "You'll be here for no longer than a week and we'll start tomorrow on your paperwork to get you out of here."

I was left, with the other Officer as a guard outside my room.

The next morning, after breakfast, Brown and his partner drove me to the office of the Chief Superintendent of Schools, in the Ugandan Education Building.

I was introduced to an East Indian clerk, named Ron Connan, who presented me with a pile of papers that he asked me to read over and sign, if I agreed with the contents.

I quickly scanned over the papers, and then perused them again. They were in essence saying: I was resigning my appointments and would not be penalized, personally or financially and had carried out my educational roles in a satisfactory manner.

I was to swear that I would not write or verbally comment on any matters taking place within the borders of Uganda, for 20 years. This included:—I was not to talk to the media or lecture on any happenings I or my family had witnessed while in Uganda.

I was never to return to Uganda, nor to write about Uganda for 40 years.

These were the major parts of the four-page document presented to me by Ron Connan.

I said, "Can I take these papers and talk then over with my wife and others?"

Connan said, "No. You either have to sign them here and now or face the consequences of."

I asked, "What consequences?"

Connan said, "Non safe passage for you and your family leaving Uganda."

I asked, "How are you in the Ministry of Education involved in giving me and my family safe passage out of here?"

Connan did not answer.

Brown handed me his pen and said, "I think you should sign, Mr. Jacques. It's your safe passage out of this country. Without signing this, you will most surely put your life, as well as that of your family's, in jeopardy. Mr. Hale recommends you sign."

I signed the document and asked for a copy of it.

Connan said, "Unfortunately, we cannot give you a transcription. The British Foreign Service will receive one. Thank you for your service to our Country of Uganda. Goodbye, Mr. Jacques and let me wish you and your family safe journey."

I was taken back to my new lodgings and instructed by Brown:—"Get some rest for the next step, tomorrow."

The next morning, Brown took me to the Ugandan Automobile Registration Office, where I met with Tom Rasmikant, an East Indian clerk.

Tom said, "Your informed Yellow Volkswagen Fastback has been sent by boxcar to Nairobi and you have to pay 200 shillings to this Ugandan office for this service."

On Brown's approval, I paid Tom the 200 shillings.

I was again taken back to my temporary residence and told again not to try to contact anyone and that tomorrow I'd be meeting with another branch of the Ugandan government.

Next morning, Brown drove me to the British Embassy, to meet with Mr. Hale. Hale said, "Mr. Jacques. We will not be taking you to any more offices of the Ugandan government, as there has been an informant that has alerted the State Research Bureau of our actions for you and you are not totally safe right now."

I asked, "What does that mean for my wife and son?"

Hale said, "They too are at risk, but not as much as you because it seems Amin has withdrawn his admiration of you and now hates you as an enemy. I think the threat to your safety is most profound and suggest you follow our instructions to a tee."

"When will I be reunited with my family?"

"As soon as it is safe. We have all of you booked on a British Airways plane, out of here, on next Saturday, at noon. You will be rejoined with your family just minutes before that plane is set to take-off."

"What am I to do till then? Can I at least phone my wife?"

"I don't think you understand the danger of such a move. You are, as of right now, a hunted man and have to lie low until we can get you, along with your wife and son, out of here safely. Do you understand?"

I said, "Where are my wife and son right now?"

"They are in a safe place. Do not worry about them. Now, do you understand?"

I nodded. Brown then drove me back to my haven where I remained until Saturday morning.

I read the Ugandan Argus with the headings: It will be Britain's responsibility:—PRESIDENT AMINS SAYS, "THE ASIANS MUST LEAVE BECAUSE THEY ARE SABOTAGING THE ECONOMY OF THE COUNTRY."

There was another heading: CANADA WILL TAKE ASIANS—Prime Minister Mr. Pierre Trudeau declined to put a quota on the amount of displaced Asians Canada would accept, but said his country would admit persons who would not normally qualify for admission.

Trudeau said, "For our part, we are prepared to offer an honorable place for Ugandan Asians to come to Canada."

Brown said, "We'll be driving through a road block on the way to Entebbe, so you'll have to ride in the trunk until we get to the airport."

"Won't they search the trunk?"

"No. We have diplomatic immunity and if they do request to open the trunk, I have a good story for them."

I arrived at the Lake Vic Hotel at 11:45 am, and with Sue and K.C. and we were shuffled into the 1st class section of the British Airways jet and airborne by noon.

<u>"SEE YA:"—A FAMILY OF FOUR ELEPHANTS,</u>

<u>LEAVE IN A HURRY,"</u>

EPILOGUE

During our years in Uganda, English was the official language, although Swahili was the prominent language among the villagers, in the then agricultural dominated country.

Most Swahili words were introduced from Arab and East Indian settlers and traders; a few by Portuguese and German colonists, and a large number from the English.

I think, the Swahili proverb that says, "When elephants fight, it is the grass that suffers," is meaningful as to what happened to the people of Uganda, in the 1970's.

The Cold War was going on and the West and the East clashed over getting a foothold in Uganda. It was a continual war of Democracy versus Communism.

The Economic War, that Amin spoke of:—between the Indigenous Africans and the Asians (East Indians), robbed the country of its productive, entrepreneurial people.

We tried our best to give you a study of life under Idi Amin and that "Pearl of Africa," as well as our Safaris in the other "Pearls:"—Kenya and Zaire.

Often, the Expatriate muzongu prefers the rural countryside to the industrial areas of Uganda, whereas the Indigenous African, in this developing country, fresh from the rough life of a village, is not likely to sympathize with this viewpoint.

To the Indigenous, the income, to sustain themselves, their immediate family and endless list of relatives, is in the urban centres, like Kampala and Jinja Town.

Most of my students came from villages. Most of them looked forward to getting a job in the city. The Uganda College of Commerce was tuitions-free and residential.

The Head of each College Department got to interview all candidates and select on a ratio of one for every five applicants.

It was usually an intense interview that lasted at least two hours.

Since there were no textbooks for any of the Departments I Headed, then I was expected to write and print up the books for the students, which I did, along with my administering to the teaching, and overseeing the post office and store staff

Sue was the Canadians in Uganda's elected representative. In that role, she set up meetings and communicated with all Canadians living in Uganda in 1972. She acted as a liaison between the Canadian government representatives and the Canadians serving in Uganda. Sue's goal was to help wherever possible and to encourage all Canadians.

Our daughter, Laura learned to appreciate Indigenous people and their culture, as well as being able to mix with young people from other nations. Her experiences in East and Central Africa helped Laura decide on following a career in Interior Design. She moved to California and married an American and has two children, Nick and Charlotte.

Our son, K.C. learned to share with others less fortunate than himself and to be a friendly and outgoing personality. On returning to Canada, K.C. went on to star as a hockey goaltender with the Provincial Rural Midget Champion Innisfail Moose and with the

Rimbey West Stars in Junior hockey. K.C. was a Central Alberta All-Star Center in high school basketball. He married and has two boys, Ben and Carson.

Kurtis is now a successful Financial Manager with World Financial Group.

When in Uganda, our concentrated efforts, were on the Indigenous African people. We were there for them and they were our number one priority.

In spite of what the people of Uganda endured, the Indigenous African Ugandans are some of the world's most open and outgoing people.

Where else would you find 30 people, pieces of luggage and chickens squeezed into a minibus taxi, called a matatu:—as it was built for a capacity of no more than 14 people, and consequently tips and sways, as it merrily moves along.

Uganda is gifted by nature with: lush foliage, rugged river gorges and silverback gorillas with biceps as big as telephone poles.

Uganda is home to the most diverse and concentrated mountain ranges of Africa with fauna that includes the endangered mountain gorilla and common chimpanzees and also the tree-climbing lion, elephant, rhinoceros, hippopotamus, giraffe, water buffalo, leopard, hyena, hartebeest, impala, warthog, okapi, crocodile, black mamba, cobra and many other animals.

The bustling capital and only city, Kampala has an African vibe so you can jump onto your boda-boda (motorcycle scooter) for a comfortable ride on red tarmac roads.

Kenya is a pearl of Africa, as the World's Safari Capital. It had a more stable government than Uganda or Zaire. We were lucky to have Canadian friends there. We loved the sandy beaches of the Indian Ocean. As one Kenyan Indigenous said, "We don't need to tan in the sun and neither do the East Indians. Just you pale musongu."

Lake Nakuru was a scenic, southwest drive through the rugged Great Rift Valley and brought us to the Masai Mara Game Reserve and its stunning array of wildlife from antelopes and lions to warthogs and zebras. Hippos, from lily pads, can lope quickly alongside the Masai River.

We experienced the local culture at a traditional Masai Village. The villager's life was simple, making their home in round boma huts constructed from mud and sticks.

Hidden in the lush, dewy Ituri Rainforest of Zaire, with its emerald vistas, were the nomadic villages of the Twa Pygmies. The Twa Pygmies were, "a pearl of Africa."

Zaire (now named, The Democratic Republic of the Congo) is full of fascinating animals, like the Okapi bull, we saw, that stood six feet at his withers. He was truly a remarkable looking animal, being reminiscent of a giraffe and a zebra.

His head was elongated like a giraffe. The muzzle and very large ears were dark colored, but the rest of his head was a pale fawn hue.

His coat was soft and of a purplish sepia color, with zebra-like stripes on his hindquarters and a more pronounced black and white bars on his legs.

The Twa Pygmies of the Ituri Rainforest were very warm and friendly to us and we were sad to hear that the ongoing civil war in their country has completely wiped them out.

Kwa heri is Goodbye, in Swahili.

When we arrived in Ottawa, Sue visited the Foreign Diseases Clinic. The doctors there had previously not experienced a person recovering from Monkey Worm.

The Head Doctor said, "It appears that all traces of the worm are gone and that Sue has recovered and will probably never put on too much weight on her frame because of the loss of most of her large intestine and some of her small intestine.

When we arrive in Calgary, I was contacted by officials at the University of Calgary and asked to meet with a group of 20 Ugandan students who were now studying at the U of C. I met with them and found all to be eager to learn and keen to return to Uganda once the war with Tanzania was over and their country returned to some semblance of normal.

The group was comprised of 20 members of the Buganda tribe. As a group, there male spokesperson, Joel said, "We are fearful of Idi Amin and his armed goons."

The four male students were studying Economics and I had taught them Accounting, when they were enrolled in Professional Studies, at U.C.C. We exchanged greetings and they were keen to learn more about Canada, and Calgary, in particular.

Sixteen of the students were female and studying Home Economics. Ten of these students had been enrolled in the Department of Home Economics I had headed at the Uganda College of Commerce. We renewed old acquaintances and friendships.

The female's spokesperson, Vera told me, "I study long, long hours to meet the standards of your country and find my professors very helpful and kind."

Vera said, "We stay in cold Canada until things settle down in Uganda."

I said, "Yes. You're used to ideal weather."

Vera answered, "We don't like the freezing cold but it is better than death."

I was also contacted by a spokesperson from the Department of Vocational Education at the University of Alberta in Edmonton.

I met with a Vocational Educational Professor, Gale at the Calgary airport and gave my opinion concerning the academic suitability of Ugandan students who wished to study in Vocational Education at the University of Alberta.

He also offered me to be an assistant to his Department at the University of Alberta that I sadly declined. It meant up-heaving our family and moving north again.

I heard, the U. of A.'s The Faculty of Commerce and Business Administration had admitted thirty Ugandan students to earn a Bachelor of Commerce and M.B.A..

In 2005, through the Canadian Humanity Foundation (CHF) of Toronto, we donated thousands of dollars to purchase medicines and medical supplies for the mothers and children of villages in Uganda. The medicines were purchased and donated by CHF, for us, to the Ugandan government for the stated purposes. Our safari ends.

Ernest Hemingway said, "It is good to have an end to journey on toward; but it is the journey itself that matters in the end." To me, journey and safari are synonymous.

OUR FAVORITE DISHES

<u>SAMOSAS</u>

BITS AND PIECES OF COOKED MEAN OR FISH IN A THIN
CRUST MADE WITH CURRIED FLOUR.

FILLING:

2-CUPS COOKED MEAT, FISH OR CHICKEN, CHOPPED
FINE

1/2-CUP ONIONS, MINCED

1/2-TEASPOON SALT

1/2 TEASPOON GROUND RED CHILI PEPPER

1/2 SMALL GREEN CHILI PEPPER, MINCED (OPTIONAL)

CRUST:

1-CUP FLOUR

1/2-TEASPOON CURRY POWDER

4 TABLESPOONS MARGARINE OR BUTTER

4 TABLESPOONS COLD WATER

SIFT FLOUR AND CURRY POWDER INTO A BOWL. WORK BUTTER OR MARGARINE IN WITH FORK OR FINGERTIPS UNTIL MIXTURE RESEMBLES COARSE MEAL. ADD WATER AND STIR TO FORM THICK DOUGH. DIVIDE DOUGH INTO 8 PARTS. ROLL OUT EACH PART INTO A VERY THIN CIRCLE. CUT CIRCLES OF DOUGH INTO QUARTERS. MIX FILLING INGREDIENTS TOGETHER AND PUT 1 TEASPOONFUL OF FILLING ON EACH QUARTER CIRCLE OF DOUGH. FOLD DOUGH OVER FILLING IN CONE SHAPE AND CRIMP EDGES WITH FORK OR FINGERS TO SEAL. BAKE IN 350 DEGREES OVEN UNTIL GOLDEN BROWN. THIS MAKES 32 SMALL SAMOSAS.

KAKLO-BANANA SNACKS

2 BANANAS

1 SMALL ONION, CHOPPED

1 TOMATO, CHOPPED

1/2 FRESH CHIL PEPPER, SEEDED AND MINCED

1/2-TEASPOON SLAT

1 TEASPOON GRATED GINER ROOT

1-CUP FLOUR

1/2-CUP WATER

USE PEANUT OIL FOR FRYING

PEEL BANANAS AND MASH. ADD CHOPPED ONION, TOMATO AND CHILI PEPPER AND MASH AGAIN. ADD SALT AND GINGER. MIX FLOUR AND WATER, THEN ADD MASH AND STIR WELL. HEAT OIL UNTIL HOT ENOUGH FOR DEEP-FRYING. DROP MIXTURE HALF-TEASPOONFUL AT A TIME INTO OIL AND FRY UNTIL GOLDEN BROWN. BALLS SHOUD BE CRISP ON THE OUTSIDE, BUT SOFT ON THE INSIDE. SERVE AS HOT OR COLD SNACKS, OR HOT WITH A MAIN DISH.

Leo Louis Jacques

COLD AVOCADO SOUP

4-CUPS CHICEN BROTH

1 TEASPOON SALT

2 RIPE AVOCADOS

1/2-TEASPOON PEPPER

4 TEASPOONS LIME JUICE

2 TEASPOONS MINCED CHIVES

PEAL AND SLICE AVOCADOS, THEN MASH. ADD TO BROTH AND STIR WELL. ADD REST OF INGREDIENTS, BLEND WELL AND CHILL. SERVE VERY COLD.

PUFF PUFFS
(RAISED DOUGH BALLS)

2-CUPS FLOUR

1 YEAST CAKE (5/8 OZ.)

1/2-CUP MILK

2 EGGS, BEATEN

1/2-CUP SUGAR

1-TEASPOON NUTMEG

1-TEASPOON VANILLA

3-CUPS PEANUT OIL FOR DEEP FAT FRYING

SIFT FLOUR INTO LARGE MIXING BOWL. DISSOLVE CRUMBLED YEAST CAKE IN ½-CUP LUKEWARM MILK. DO NOT LET MILK GET HOT. COMBINE BEATEN EGGS, SUGAR, NUTMEG, VANILLA AND YEAST MIXTURE TO FORM SOFT DOUGH. COVER BOWL WITH THIN CLEAN CLOTH AND SET IN A WARM PLACE TO RISE. LET DOUGH RISE UNTIL DOUBLE IN BULK (AN HOUR OR MORE). HEAT OIL IN HEAVY POT TO DEEP FAT FRYING (375 DEG.) TEMPERATURE. USING TEASPOON, SHAPE DOUGH INTO SMALL BALLS AND DROP INTO BOILING OIL A FEW AT A TIME. DIP TEASPOON IN COLD WATER AFTER EACH

SHAPING TO KEEP DOUGH FROM STICKING. FRY BALLS TO GOLDEN BROWN. REMOVE WITH SLOTTED SPOON. DRAIN ON PAPER TOWELS. SPRINKLE WITH SUGAR AND SERVE HOT. MAKES TWO DOZEN

OROMBO

JUICE OF SIX ORANGES OR THREE GRAPEFRUIT

4-CUPS HOT WATER

4 TABLESPOONS SUGAR.

PUT JUICE IN PITCHER. ADD WATER AND SUGAR. COOL. SERVE WITH ICE CUBES. (GIN, RUM OR VODKA MAY BE ADDED.)

SWAHILI RIDDLES

Don't expect to be lucky all the time.

Oh Lord, save us from the evil ones.

Your bad words against me incite others against you.

Small things make up big things.

Hate me but I will still tell the truth.

Good Intentions need tangible results.

Rushing isn't always good.

A person playing with a razor gets cut

Don't be nosy about me.

God judges everything: He welcomes.

Don't joke too much, or anger will arise.

I live as I can afford, not as you wish.

I thought of you as a pearl, but you are a poison.

A person becomes bad when he harms you.

It's wise to treat everyone equally and with respect.

There's no escaping one's fate.

Good moral character is better than material wealth.

Lord save me from poisonous plots.

An eye is sharper than a razor.

Make judgment based on both pearl and poisons.

A quiet lion catches its prey.

One does not throw away a stick until after the snake has gone.

CPSIA information can be obtained at www.ICGtesting.com
Printed in the USA
LVOW130645050613

336931LV00002B/7/P

9 781481 732727